The Japanese Economy

by Kayo Kobayashi

JN094940

Translated by Giles Murray

IBC パブリッシング

はじめに

　ラダーシリーズは、「はしご（ladder）」を使って一歩一歩上を目指すように、学習者の実力に合わせ、無理なくステップアップできるよう開発された英文リーダーのシリーズです。

　リーディング力をつけるためには、繰り返したくさん読むこと、いわゆる「多読」がもっとも効果的な学習法であると言われています。多読では、「1.速く　2.訳さず英語のまま　3.なるべく辞書を使わず」に読むことが大切です。スピードを計るなど、速く読むよう心がけましょう（たとえばTOEIC®テストの音声スピードはおよそ1分間に150語です）。そして1語ずつ訳すのではなく、英語を英語のまま理解するくせをつけるようにします。こうして読み続けるうちに語感がついてきて、だんだんと英語が理解できるようになるのです。まずは、ラダーシリーズの中からあなたのレベルに合った本を選び、少しずつ英文に慣れ親しんでください。たくさんの本を手にとるうちに、英文書がすらすら読めるようになってくるはずです。

《本シリーズの特徴》

- 中学校レベルから中級者レベルまで5段階に分かれています。自分に合ったレベルからスタートしてください。

- クラシックから現代文学、ノンフィクション、ビジネスと幅広いジャンルを扱っています。あなたの興味に合わせてタイトルを選べます。

- 巻末のワードリストで、いつでもどこでも単語の意味を確認できます。レベル1、2では、文中の全ての単語が、レベル3以上は中学校レベル外の単語が掲載されています。

- カバーにヘッドホーンマークのついているタイトルは、オーディオ・サポートがあります。ウェブから購入／ダウンロードし、リスニング教材としても併用できます。

《使用語彙について》

レベル1：中学校で学習する単語約1000語

レベル2：レベル1の単語＋使用頻度の高い単語約300語

レベル3：レベル1の単語＋使用頻度の高い単語約600語

レベル4：レベル1の単語＋使用頻度の高い単語約1000語

レベル5：語彙制限なし

CONTENTS

Foreword .... *vi*

PART ONE:
  A Brief History of
  the Japanese Economy *1*

PART TWO:
  Structure of the Japanese Economy *15*

PART THREE:
  Japan in the International Economy *33*

PART FOUR:
  The Japanese Economy at
  a Turning Point *47*

PART FIVE:
  The Japanese Economy in
  the 21st Century *69*

Word List *92*

Foreword

This book explains the basics of the Japanese economy in simple English.

It first looks back at the history of the Japanese economy from the end of World War II. It starts with Japan's recovery from ruin after the war. It then shows how Japan became an economic superpower through rapid economic growth. Next, it covers the "bubble economy" and the collapse of the bubble. Finally, it analyzes the stagnation that followed.

The book also describes the structure of the Japanese economy. It sums up the features of Japanese corporate management (or the "Japanese-style management system"). It looks at the role of the bureaucrats who supported Japan's rapid economic growth. And it examines the major industries of Japan and explains why they are highly competitive in the world market.

The book also examines the position of the Japanese economy on the world stage. It examines issues that have caused political and social problems, such as moving factories overseas to cope with strong trade friction and the rising yen exchange rate.

I explain the current state of the Japanese economy and the various problems it is facing. I underline how the economy—with challenges that include huge fiscal deficits, a decreasing birthrate and an aging population, and environmental problems—finds itself at a major turning point. I also examine various policies designed to address these problems.

Last of all, I look at trends in the Japanese economy since the start of the 21st century. I explain the impact of the structural reforms of the government of Junichiro Koizumi, the 2008 financial crisis, and the 2011 Great East Japan Earthquake on the Japanese economy. I also touch upon the economic policies (known as Abenomics) that were put in place by the government of Shinzo Abe, and the pandemic of 2020.

I wrote this book about topics that often come up in newspapers, in magazines, and on television news.

It should be easy to read even for people who have never studied economics, who know nothing about the basics of economics, or who have stayed away from the subject because it is not "their thing." People who know some economics will learn how to better express economic concepts in English and master English economic terms.

The economy has a great impact on our everyday lives. I hope that reading this book will help increase your familiarity with and interest in the Japanese economy.

Kayo Kobayashi

PART ONE

A Brief History of the Japanese Economy

読みはじめる前に

目を通しておくと、この章が読みやすくなる経済用語です。

agricultural and land reform	農地改革
Bank of Japan（BOJ）	日本銀行，日銀
basic industry	基幹産業
capital investment	設備投資
central bank governor	中央銀行総裁
company men	会社人間
consumer durable	耐久消費財
coordinated intervention	協調介入
dollar-denominated assets	ドル建て資産
economic boom	好景気，好況
economic superpower	経済大国
Economic White Paper	経済白書
finance minister	財務大臣，大蔵大臣
financial institution	金融機関
five advanced nations	先進5カ国（G5）
foreign exchange market	外国為替市場
gross national product（GNP）	国民総生産
Income Doubling Plan	所得倍増計画
Iwato Boom	岩戸景気
Izanagi Boom	いざなぎ景気
Jimmu Boom	神武景気
Labor Standards Law	労働基準法，労働三法
land myth	土地神話

land-holding tax	地価税，土地保有税
land taxation	土地税制
Lost Decade	失われた10年
mass-production	大量生産
Minamata Disease	水俣病
national income	国民所得
Nikkei Stock Average	日経平均株価
Nixon Shock	ニクソン・ショック
official discount rate	公定歩合
oil crisis	オイルショック，石油危機
passionate salaried employees	猛烈社員
personal consumption	個人消費
Plaza Accord	プラザ合意
postwar reconstruction	戦後復興
rapid economic growth	高度経済成長
savings rate	貯蓄率
three excesses	3つの過剰。excess capital investment（過剰設備投資），excess employment（過剰雇用），excessive debt（過剰債務）
three sacred treasures	三種の神器。テレビ，洗濯機，冷蔵庫のこと。
U.S. government bond	米国債
white-collar worker	サラリーマン，事務系の仕事をする人
Yom Kippur War	第四次中東戦争，ヨーム・キップール・ウォー

Postwar Reconstruction

Defeat in World War II hit Japan hard. Repeated air raids destroyed factories and production facilities and nearly annihilated industry.

After the war, the policies of the Allied Occupation Army set Japan on the road to reconstruction and democratization. The first step the Occupation Army took was to break up the *zaibatsu* (like Mitsui and Mitsubishi), which had controlled the prewar Japanese economy. Secondly, it implemented agricultural and land reforms to establish an owner-farmer system. Thirdly, it enacted the Labor Standards Law to help democratize labor.

The Priority Production System was one policy that helped the postwar Japanese economy recover. This system directed Japan's limited capital and resources into the production of primary materials. These primary materials served as an engine for the whole economy. The Priority Production System first targeted basic industries such as coal, iron and steel, and then other industries such as food and fertilizer.

The Korean War broke out in June 1950 and lasted until July 1953. During the war, Japan received large orders from the U.S. Army for blankets, trucks, steel, and other war materials. As a result, Japan's exports grew rapidly.

These special orders for Korean War goods started the full recovery of Japan's economy. All the economic indices, such as industrial production, personal consumption, private-sector investment, and the gross national product (GNP), returned to their prewar levels. Now the process of recovery from the postwar chaos was almost complete. The economy was entering into a rapid growth period.

The 1956 Economic White Paper declared: "The postwar period is now over."

Rapid Growth *(See Fig. 1-1)*

After the postwar recovery, the Japanese economy grew strongly from the mid-1950s to the early 1970s. This rapid growth was due to a large supply of cheap, high-quality labor, a high savings rate, and a strong drive by corporations to invest.

Soon after becoming prime minister in 1960, Hayato Ikeda announced the Income Doubling Plan. Under the plan, economic growth of around 9%

for 10 years would result in a doubling of GNP and national income. In fact, the economy grew at an average of 10.9%, well above the Ikeda target. Japan was on the road to becoming an economic superpower.

In 1964, Tokyo held the Olympic Games. Development for the games included the Tokaido bullet train and the expressways. In 1968, Japan's GNP ranked No. 2 in the world. The hardworking white-collar workers, often called "company men" (*kaishaningen*) or "passionate salaried employees" (*mouretsushain*), were one reason behind this high economic growth.

Fig. 1-1 Changes in real GDP rate (%)

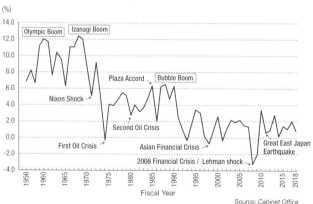

Source: *Cabinet Office*

During the period of rapid economic growth, there were several large-scale economic booms. The Jimmu Boom (1955–1957) and the Iwato Boom (1958–1961) were driven mainly by capital investment from the heavy-chemicals industry. In contrast, exports of Japanese goods drove the next boom: the Izanagi Boom of 1965–1970.

During the period of rapid economic growth, consumer durables became more widespread thanks to a fall in prices brought about by mass production. In the late 1950s, the television, washing machine, and refrigerator were called the "three sacred treasures" of consumer products. In the late 1960s, the car, the color television, and the air conditioner (the three Cs) became the "three *new* sacred treasures."

However, pollution-related problems, such as Minamata Disease and Itai-Itai Disease in the late 1960s, showed that rapid economic growth had its negative side, too.

In 1971, U.S. President Nixon stopped the convertibility of the U.S. dollar into gold. This was called the "Nixon Shock." This forced the yen exchange rate up. Next, the 1973 Yom Kippur War in the Middle East started the first oil crisis and caused the price of oil to rise. These external shocks brought Japan's rapid growth to an end. The economy grew at slower and steadier rates from this point on.

The Bubble Economy *(See Fig. 1-2)*

The boom of the late 1980s and early 1990s was driven by a bubble caused by speculative fever in real estate and stocks, known as the "bubble economy."

The 1985 Plaza Accord triggered the bubble economy. Finance ministers and central bank governors of the five advanced nations (G5) assembled for the Plaza meeting at the request of the United States, which was suffering a trade deficit brought about by the strong dollar. At the meeting, the G5 leaders agreed that participating countries would carry out coordinated intervention in the foreign exchange markets to bring the value of the dollar down.

As a result of the Plaza Accord, the yen appreciated rapidly. On the Tokyo market, the yen had been trading at 242 yen to the U.S. dollar prior to the Plaza Accord. By the end of 1985, the yen had become so strong that it passed the 200-yen-to-the-dollar level. The appreciation of the yen created a foreign-exchange loss in dollar-denominated assets such as U.S. government bonds. This drove capital back to Japan where there was no foreign-exchange risk. The official discount rate was lowered five times by February 1987 in order to help the competitiveness of domestic exporters and manufacturers, which had fallen due to the strong yen. The official discount rate hit 2.5%. This was the lowest level since the end of World War II.

This process led to a boom in domestic investment in real estate and stocks. Stock and land prices both rose, but land prices rose particularly high because

Fig. 1-2 Changes in USD/JPY

of the "land myth"—the belief that land prices would never fall. Banks expanded their loans with land as collateral. The rise in the value of assets and the resulting unrealized profits only encouraged individuals and corporations to invest more. Land-sharking became a social problem and the mad buying of overseas assets caught a lot of public attention.

The Lost Decade

Japan's bubble economy collapsed at the start of the 1990s. The government and the Bank of Japan (BOJ) caused the collapse by trying to cool the bubble down.

In 1989, the Bank of Japan changed to a tight-money policy and, in 1990, raised the official discount rate to 6%. Also in 1990, the Ministry of Finance requested that banks restrict their financing of property assets and the government introduced a new system of land taxation (including a land-holding tax) in hopes of destroying the "land myth." The Nikkei Stock Average and the price of land fell from their highs in December 1989 and autumn 1990, respectively.

After the bubble, the Japanese economy entered a long period of stagnation. The economy picked up several times during the 1990s, but a full recovery never happened.

Financial institutions ended up with very large levels of non-performing loans as a result of the collapse in share prices and land values. Corporations suffered from the "three excesses": excess capital investment, excess employment, and excessive debt. Corporate earnings fell, the government budget situation got worse, and unemployment rose. It was one gloomy piece of news after another.

Though the government did not officially accept the fact, the Japanese economy had fallen into a deflationary spiral: a vicious circle where falling corporate profits lead to declining capital investment, falling employment, falling wages, stagnating consumption, and then to further declines in corporate profits.

Government negligence and the failure of government economic policy (such as putting off dealing with the non-performing loan issue) were major causes of the prolonged economic stagnation. This period is called the "Lost Decade."

Non-Performing Loans

During the bubble period, banks lent out vast amounts of money to companies, taking land and stock as collateral. However, once the bubble collapsed and the economy stagnated, many companies started experiencing financial difficulties. They were unable to repay even the interest on their loans, let alone the principal. Because of the drop in value of this land and stock, banks were unable to recover their loans. Thus, banks ended up with huge amounts of non-performing loans on their books. According to a 2002 statement from the Financial Services Agency, the total value of non-performing loans held by banks was 43.2 trillion yen.

Non-performing loans became a drag on the Japanese economy and how to dispose of them became a major political issue. The government instructed banks to conduct a strict "self-assessment" of their assets and keep sufficient reserves to cover any losses. On their accounting sheets, banks had to calculate expected losses for three types of borrowers: (1) "borrowers likely to go bankrupt," (2) "effectively bankrupt borrowers," and (3) "actual bankrupt borrowers." The banks were legally required to keep reserves for loan losses based on the categories of borrowers of non-performing loans. The Japanese tax code does not allow banks to write off loans unless a company actually goes bankrupt, and thus, the increase in reserves required for loan losses reduced the profitability of banks.

In this way, the non-performing loan problem was gradually solved. The balance of non-performing loans, which stood at 17.9 trillion yen in 2005, shrank to 13.3 trillion yen in 2006. As the banks began to dispose of their non-performing loans, the Japanese economy finally began to show signs of revival and to emerge from a long slump.

PART TWO

Structure of
the Japanese Economy

読みはじめる前に

目を通しておくと、この章が読みやすくなる経済用語です。

administrative guidance	行政指導
board of directors	取締役会
capital trading practice	資本取引慣行
client company	取引先
community with a shared destiny	運命共同体
company labor union	企業組合
corporate financing	企業金融
cross-shareholdings	（企業間の）株式持ち合い
deregulation	規制緩和, 自由化
digital consumer electronics	デジタル家電
direct financing	直接金融
electrical machinery	電気機械
electronics technology	エレクトロニクス技術
equity ratio	自己資本比率
export industry	輸出産業
go bankrupt	倒産する
governance function	ガバナンス機能
growth industry	成長産業
indirect financing	間接金融
industrial policy	産業政策
"intelligent" consumer electronics	情報家電
"just-in-time production" system	ジャスト・イン・タイム方式

kanban system	カンバン方式
labor issue	労働問題
lifetime employment	終身雇用
main bank system	メインバンクシステム
management system	経営管理システム
manufacturer	製造業者, メーカー
Ministry of Economy, Trade and Industry（METI）	経済産業省
Ministry of Finance（MOF）	財務省, 大蔵省
Ministry of International Trade and Industry（MITI）	通商産業省, 通産省
natural resource	自然資源, 天然資源
personnel system	人事制度
processing trade	加工貿易
production management system	生産管理システム
production process	生産工程
production system	生産システム
raw material	原材料
retirement	（定年）退職
seniority system	年功序列制度
silent shareholder	物言わぬ株主, サイレント株主
trade liberalization	貿易自由化

The Japanese Management System
One: Lifetime Employment, the Seniority System, and Company Labor Unions

There are some unique features of Japanese corporations that lie behind the economy's strong development after World War II, such as lifetime employment, the seniority system, and company labor unions. These are sometimes called the "three sacred treasures" of the Japanese management system.

Lifetime employment means that employees are hired straight after graduation and continue to work at the same company until retirement. Employees have no worries about losing their jobs, so they can feel secure and focus on their work.

The seniority system means that staff are promoted and receive pay increases based upon their length of service at a company. This encourages employees to stay with the company for the long term. Since they are not exposed to excessive competition within the company and their conditions improve steadily every year, workers usually choose to stay at the same company.

In the chaos after World War II, Japanese

corporations experienced a serious labor shortage. As a result, a variety of new personnel systems were implemented in an effort to retain workers. The lifetime employment and seniority systems were two of these.

There was a family-like harmony at the Japanese corporation. The company and the employee held deep feelings of trust for each other. Employees developed a sense of loyalty and love for their company. This, in turn, motivated them to work hard. Companies fostered a sense of belonging to the group that led to successful teamwork. This teamwork had a very positive effect on corporate results.

On top of this, Japanese employees organized into company labor unions. This meant that union members would lose their jobs if the company they worked for went bankrupt. That is why labor disputes never got out of control (except for during a brief period after the war). Labor issues were dealt with in a manner suited to the situation at each individual company and labor-management relations were basically harmonious.

As a result of the "three sacred treasures," the Japanese company and its employees formed a "community with a shared destiny." The strong bond between management and employees contributed a great deal to corporate growth and the development of the Japanese economy as a whole.

The Japanese Management System
Two: Cross-Shareholdings *(See Fig. 2-1)*

Cross-holding shares is a capital trading practice unique to Japan. As a result of the postwar breakup of the *zaibatsu*, large amounts of *zaibatsu* shares were released onto the market and there were many

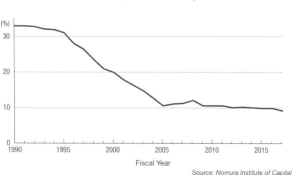

Fig. 2-1 Cross-Holdings as a Percentage of
Market Capitalization of Japanese Stocks

Fiscal Year

Source: *Nomura Institute of Capital Markets Research*

corporate takeovers. In self-defense, companies "cross-held" each other's shares. Financial institutions like banks, non-financial companies, and other companies with close business relationships, held each other's shares to try to keep a stable shareholding structure.

Particularly among manufacturers, it became common to form *keiretsu*. These are vertically integrated industrial groupings based on cross-shareholding. A company would group itself with its most important trading partners to maintain long-term trading relationships. Within the *keiretsu*, companies would jointly develop products and collaborate on production processes, thus achieving high quality at low cost.

The *keiretsu*'s loyal shareholders never complained about the company's management policy even when the company's results were poor and dividends low. That is why they were called "silent shareholders." Since "silent shareholders" never sold their shares, the overall number of floating shares on the market was low. This stopped stock prices from ever falling too much.

Other countries attacked the cross-shareholding

system for being "closed" and "not transparent." The system gradually started to come apart in the 1990s. The movement to sell off cross-held shares and take profits has been particularly common among financial institutions, which have been eager to improve their deteriorating earnings and strengthen their equity ratios.

The Japanese Management System
Three: The Main Bank System

Japanese corporate financing depends a great deal on bank loans or indirect financing. The "main bank" system is one of the main features of Japan's indirect financing system.

A main bank fulfills the following conditions. It is the main provider of loans to a client company. It is a major shareholder in the client company. And it has a direct, personal relationship with the client company and often supplies the client company with executives and other staff.

Main banks take on the role of governance and keep an eye on the management of their client companies. In most cases, a Japanese company's board of directors is made up of senior staff that have been promoted from within the organization. The other major shareholders are "silent shareholders" and let the main bank run the company.

In this context, the main bank plays an extremely important role. If its client company has financial problems, the main bank increases oversight, takes over the company's management, and directs the restructuring of the company. Because companies work hard to avoid this sort of intervention by the main bank, the main bank system encourages efficiency in management. And, since main banks take a leading role in rescuing companies in crisis by offering emergency loans, they help the financial stability of Japan, too.

Recently, questions have been raised about the effectiveness of the "main bank" system. Particularly at big companies, the level of direct financing from capital markets is rising while cross-shareholding is decreasing. As the governance function of the main banks shrinks, the importance of active governance by shareholders has greatly increased.

The Japanese Management System
Four: Kanban and Kaizen

Japanese industry has become internationally competitive as a result of daily efforts and innovations to improve the production process. The most famous examples of these are kanban and kaizen. Both originated in Toyota Motor's production management system.

The kanban system is also called the "just-in-time production" system in English. It works like this. A worker slips a plate (called a *kanban*) in between the stock of parts piled up for production. The mold number of the part, its name, and the quantity needed are written on the plate. As the parts get used, the plate rises to the top of the pile. When the worker sees the plate, he sends it to the parts manufacturer as if it were an order slip. By getting parts and materials in the precise quantity, exactly when they are needed, stocks of parts and products can be kept at the lowest level possible.

Kaizen means continuously working to produce cheaper, higher-quality products and deliver them on time. Workers suggest and help implement ways to get rid of excess burden, waste, and inefficiency in the production process. One small improvement after another gradually leads to huge improvements in final results.

Toyota started the practices of kanban and kaizen, but many other Japanese companies have since adopted the same methods. Now, kanban and kaizen have become standard production management methods in Japan. The Japanese manufacturing industry has become internationally competitive because of efficient production systems like these that help produce high-quality products at low cost.

Bureaucrats and the Private Sector

Government industrial policy played a very important role in helping Japan's economy achieve high growth.

After World War II, the government implemented an economic planning policy with the aim of reviving and strengthening Japan's productive power. The government rationed important business resources such as raw materials and capital, giving priority to core industries like coal, iron and steel, and electric-power generation. The government also directed the industrial revival by limiting market competition, giving administrative guidance, and implementing other policies.

MITI (the Ministry of International Trade and Industry, now called METI, the Ministry of Economy, Trade and Industry) decided which industries were strategically important and implemented policies to develop these behind protective barriers. The Ministry of Finance (MOF) provided financial support to these industries.

In the rapid growth period of the 1960s, strategic industries shifted to consumer durables such as automobiles and home appliances. In the 1980s, these changed again—to computers, semiconductors, and electronics.

Government policies had a strong influence on corporate activity. There was a popular theory that Japan functioned like a single, huge company (and Japan was sometimes referred to as "Japan Inc.").

Japanese industries that became competitive through protective development policies and close government cooperation increased exports, particularly to the United States. This helped the Japanese economy achieve rapid growth.

The present wave of trade liberalization and deregulation has increasingly limited the role of industrial policy.

The Growth of World-Leading Industries
(See Fig. 2-2)

Defeat in World War II hit Japan hard. Because Japan had few natural resources, it had to develop its economy through what is called the "processing trade." The processing trade involves importing raw materials, processing them at home, and then exporting them as finished products. At present, Japan is the world leader in the production of automobiles, electrical machinery, and appliances, which are types of processing trade.

Japan's automobile industry passed the United States in production-unit terms in 1980 to become No. 1 in the world. The first oil crisis helped Japan's auto industry by creating more demand for small, fuel-efficient cars in the United States. As Japanese cars became more popular, exports grew.

Japan's production system (as represented by

Toyota Motors' kanban and kaizen systems) was highly productive and helped introduce new models with shorter lead times. Japanese cars became known for high quality at low cost. The success of the industry had a huge impact on the Japanese economy at large because the auto industry is a key industry with a wide network of smaller automobile-related industries.

Fig. 2-2 Changes in Export Value by Major Industry Sectors

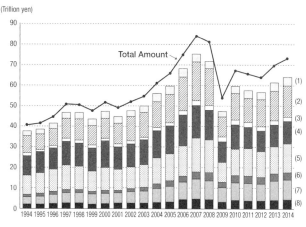

(Trillion yen)

Total Amount

(1) Precision Equipment   (4) Electric Appliances   (7) Chemical and Plastic Products
(2) Automotive   (5) General Machinery   (8) Others
(3) Transportation Machinery   (6) Iron and Steel

Source: *Ministry of Economy, Trade and Industry*

Electrical machinery and appliances also contributed to the development of the Japanese economy. After the war, electronics technology originally developed for the military was switched to civilian use in products like radios and televisions. In addition, new technology was imported from abroad. The electrical goods business grew because the Japanese had a natural talent for turning technology to consumer-product purposes. This let them mass-produce high-quality, low-priced products.

In the domestic market, booms in the production of the "three sacred treasures" and pocket calculators increased demand for home electric appliances and electronic components. Exports rose too, and Japanese-made electric appliances and audio-visual products like televisions and radios enjoyed a large market share worldwide. Japan introduced original products as well, like the Sony Walkman. Digital consumer electronics and "intelligent" consumer electronics were seen as new growth areas. There was fierce R&D competition among the different electronics companies.

New Growth Industries: Video Games, Comics, and Cartoons

Video games, comic books (*manga*), and cartoons (*anime*) have become Japan's major new export industries. Japan reportedly makes about 60% of the cartoons now being broadcast on television worldwide.

Dragon Ball and *Pokémon*, for example, which were first broadcast in the United States, went on to become worldwide hits. *Doraemon* remains a long-term favorite. *Spirited Away*, a feature-length animated film directed by Hayao Miyazaki, won global acclaim. Meanwhile, in the video game industry, Japanese companies like Sony Computer Entertainment and Nintendo are major trendsetters.

The Japanese video game, comic book, and cartoon industries are closely connected. Japanese comic book production boomed in the 1960s. Cartoons developed from comic books grew with the spread of television and VCRs. Home video games made their debut in the 1980s and grew rapidly during the 1990s with the evolution of personal computers. As game machines and software grew more sophisticated, they reached every corner of the world. Today, Japanese companies hold the majority of the world market for these goods.

Japanese video games, comic books, and cartoons are imaginative, emotionally sophisticated, and technologically advanced. Their variety has increased because of intense competition in the domestic market. This also explains why they have won such broad success outside Japan.

PART THREE

Japan in the International Economy

読みはじめる前に

目を通しておくと、この章が読みやすくなる経済用語です。

advanced nation	先進国
chemical products	化学製品
competitiveness	競争力
division of labor	分業体制
domestic consumption [demand]	国内消費，内需
Economic Partnership Agreement（EPA）	経済連携協定
exchange rate	為替レート
exchange-rate risk	為替リスク
export-led economy	輸出主導型経済
finished goods [products]	完成品
hollowing out of industry	産業の空洞化
increasing domestic demand	内需拡大
interest rate	金利，利率
international competitiveness	国際競争力
Japan-U.S. Framework for New Economic Partnership	日米包括経済協議
political issue	政治問題
rate of real economic growth	実質経済成長率
return of Okinawa to Japan	沖縄返還
semlconductor	半導体

strong dollar	ドル高
strong yen	円高
strong-yen recession	円高不況
Structural Impediments Initiative (**SII**)	日米構造協議
subcontractor	下請業者
tariff	関税 (率)
textile industry	繊維産業
torrential exports	集中豪雨的輸出
trade deficit	貿易赤字
trade friction	貿易摩擦
trade problem	貿易問題
trade surplus	輸出超過額
trading partner	貿易相手国
Trans-Pacific Partnership (**TPP**)	環太平洋パートナーシップ協定
high-value-added	高付加価値の, 付加価値の高い
weak dollar	ドル安
weak yen	円安

The Export-Led Economy

Until the mid-1980s, Japan achieved economic growth through an export-led economy. After the war, the government made efforts to raise the international competitiveness of Japan's manufacturing sector through industrial policy and other measures. Since Japan has few natural resources, the aim was to develop the economy through the "processing trade." The processing trade is the business of importing raw materials, processing them, and then exporting them as finished products.

Japanese low-priced, high-quality products made big inroads into foreign markets, particularly the United States. During the period of rapid economic growth, Japanese exports grew twice as fast as world exports on average. At first, Japan's main exports were textile products. Gradually, exports changed to large-scale heavy industrial and chemical products like iron and steel and shipbuilding materials. Exports then shifted to machinery, electronic equipment, automobiles, and home electronic appliances.

Japanese exporters focused a great deal of energy on a specific product type for a very short period of time. Thus, importing countries sometimes called Japanese exports "torrential exports." Trade friction sometimes resulted when these exports damaged the industries of importing countries. As Japan's international competitiveness rose and its exports expanded, trade problems became a political issue.

Trade Friction

Trade friction caused by huge trade surpluses became a serious problem, particularly with the United States.

Textiles were the first trade issue to cause problems between Japan and the United States. The American textile industry was suffering as a result of increasing competition from imported Japanese textiles and so the U.S. government asked Japan to restrict the export of textiles. The two governments coordinated over the issue and settled the dispute after Japan imposed voluntary export controls in exchange for the return of Okinawa to Japan in 1972.

In the 1970s, exports like iron and steel, televisions, VCRs, and machine tools caused more trade friction. In the 1980s, the focus was on cars and semiconductors. At one time, Japan alone accounted for one quarter of the U.S. trade deficit.

Various measures were taken to reduce trade friction. The Plaza Accord was signed in 1985. This led to a realignment of the currency exchange rates between advanced nations. As a result, the dollar fell and the yen rose. In 1988, imports of beef and oranges were liberalized, and the drive to open up Japanese markets broadened. In 1989, the Structural Impediments Initiative (SII) was launched to further open Japanese markets to foreign products. In 1993, SII was renamed the Japan-U.S. Framework for New Economic Partnership and involved discussions on the deregulation of Japan and the further opening of Japanese markets.

The Strong Yen and Overseas Production
(See Fig. 3-1)

In September 1985, the Plaza Accord was signed. As a result, there was a sudden change from a strong dollar and weak yen to a weak dollar and strong yen. The exchange rate, which was 242 yen to the dollar before the Plaza Accord, rose to 200 yen to the dollar by the year-end. By the beginning of 1988, it had reached 128 yen to the dollar.

Because of the rapid rise in the yen's value, Japan fell into a strong-yen recession. The rate of real economic growth fell from 5.2% in 1985 to 2.6% in 1986. In yen-based terms, exports dropped significantly and the export and manufacturing sectors lost competitiveness.

To deal with the rise of the yen, the government implemented a policy of increasing domestic demand by lowering interest rates. The official

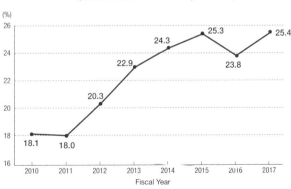

Fig. 3-1 Overseas Production Ratio in Manufacturing
(based on all domestic corporations)

Source: *Ministry of Economy, Trade and Industry*

discount rate was cut five times by February 1987, from 5% originally to 2.5%, the lowest rate in the postwar period. This easy-money policy stimulated investment in plant and information technology.

At the same time, since the rise of the yen made it harder for companies to manufacture and export from Japan, they started moving their factories overseas. Switching to local production in foreign countries was an attempt to avoid exchange-rate risk. Moving factories overseas was not limited to major manufacturers of finished goods but also included parts suppliers and subcontractors.

As the manufacturing sector moved more and more factories overseas, the "hollowing out of industry" meant shrinking domestic production and falling employment.

The Rise of China *(See Fig. 3-2)*

The Chinese economy continues to develop at an extremely rapid pace and China is becoming an ever more important trading partner for Japan. China became Japan's largest trading partner for the first time in 2004, with total trade (the combined value of imports and exports) hitting 22.2 trillion yen. (Japan's total trade with the United States in the same year was 20.48 trillion yen.) China has remained Japan's largest trading partner ever since. Japan is China's second-largest trading partner after the United States and Japanese businesses have more overseas outposts in China than in any other country. The economic relationship between the two countries is a very tight one.

Fig. 3-2 Changes in the Composition of Major Regions in Japan's Total Trade

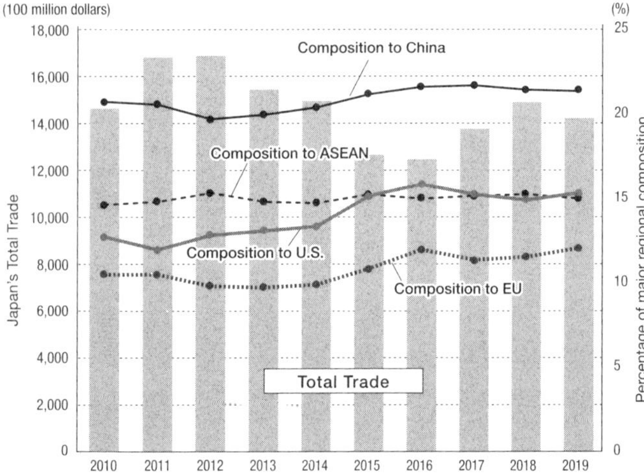

Source: Japan External Trade Organization (JETRO)

China's domestic consumption continues to grow. The Chinese market is an enormous market that Japanese businesses must seek to address. In recent years, Japan is exporting all sorts of things to China. As well as high-value-added finished goods, Japan is exporting raw materials, high-tech components and manufacturing equipment. China is assembling these to increase its own exports of finished goods. You might say that Japan and China have between them established their own structural division of labor.

With the growth of the Chinese economy, the number of Chinese tourists visiting Japan has risen. The number of Chinese visitors to Japan outstripped the number of Japanese visitors to China for the first time in 2015. Accounting for 30% of all foreign visitors to Japan, Chinese tourists represent the largest single group. Chinese tourists can be seen buying vast quantities of Japan-made goods all around the country in a phenomenon known as *bakugai* (explosive buying).

There are occasional flare-ups in the relationship of the two countries caused by such things as territorial disputes and the "history problem" (different interpretations of history), but in purely economic terms China will remain an important country for Japan. The economic interdependence of the two countries is only deepening.

Economic Partnership Agreements (EPA)

From the 2000s, Japan has taken a proactive approach toward signing economic partnership agreements (EPA). Since it concluded its first EPA with Singapore in 2002, Japan now has EPAs with 18 countries and regions, chiefly in ASEAN countries.

An EPA is an agreement designed to broaden and strengthen the economic relationship between two or more countries by promoting the liberalization and streamlining of trade and investment. With the signing of an EPA, exporting companies can expect to maintain or reinforce their export competitiveness through the introduction of measures such as tariff reduction. EPAs establish an environment that make it easy for companies with investment assets overseas or that provide services overseas to further develop their business.

The EPA that garnered the most attention was the Trans-Pacific Partnership, or TPP. Negotiations were conducted between a total of 12 countries including Australia, Brunei, Canada, Chile, Malaysia, Mexico, New Zealand, Peru, Singapore, the United States and Vietnam, in addition to Japan. The Trump administration announced that the United States would withdraw in 2017, but the remaining 11 countries continued to negotiate and the TPP-11 came into effect in 2018.

As a result of the agreement, tariffs are being eliminated for 82.3% of all categories of agricultural produce and, eventually, for 99.9% of categories of industrial products. Together the 11 countries, which have around 500 million people, account for roughly 6% of the world's population. Meanwhile, their combined GDP is equivalent to 13% of global GDP. The advantage for Japan is that it can enjoy the profits that result from the economic growth of the signatory countries, first and foremost the fast-growing countries of Southeast Asia. The Japanese government reckons that the TPP-11 will boost Japanese GDP by 7.8 trillion yen annually and lead to the creation of jobs for 460,000 people.

PART FOUR

The Japanese Economy at a Turning Point

読みはじめる前に

目を通しておくと、この章が読みやすくなる経済用語です。

aging society	高齢化社会
asset deflation	資産デフレ
birth rate	出生率
budget deficit	財政赤字
central government	中央政府
convoy system	護送船団方式
corporate profit	企業収益
credit risk	信用リスク
deflation	デフレーション
deflationary spiral	デフレスパイラル
destruction of the ozone layer	オゾン層破壊
financial product	金融商品
fiscal reform	財政改革
fiscal stimulus package	財政刺激策
global warming	地球温暖化
government bond	国債
government deficit	財政赤字，政府赤字
greenhouse gases	温室効果ガス
human resources	人材，人的資源
Japan premium	ジャパン・プレミアム
Japanese Big Bang	日本型ビッグバン

Kyoto Protocol	京都議定書
liquidity risk	流動性リスク
local government	地方自治体，地方政府
non-performing loans	不良債権
non-tariff barrier	非関税障壁
oversupply	供給過剰
Paris Agreement	パリ協定
price destruction	価格破壊
price war	値下げ競争，価格競争
private sector	民間企業［部門］
redemption	償還
social security system [program]	社会保障制度
stagnation	停滞，低迷
subsidiary company	子会社，系列会社
subsidy	助成金，補助金
tax revenue	税収，歳入
tax sources	税源
triple reform	三位一体の改革

Deflation

The Japanese economy fell into deflation in the second half of the 1990s and proved unable to conquer it for the next 20 years. Japan is the only country to have experienced such long-term deflation in the postwar period.

Japan's deflation is the result of asset deflation. The fall in stock prices and property values brought on by the collapse of the bubble economy caused this asset deflation, which gave birth to banks' non-performing loans. The banks were unable to deal with their bad loan problem fast enough and the economy soon fell into a vicious circle of financial trouble.

At the same time, there was also general price deflation. This was the result of oversupply caused by excess capital investment during the bubble period and the fall in consumption after the collapse of the bubble.

In the mid-1990s, the term "price destruction" was much in fashion. There was a rapid increase in the number of new businesses using low prices as a sales weapon, such as for men's clothing, home appliances, and food. When existing businesses fought back, a price war broke out. This caused a further fall in prices. Also, as China's economy grew, Japan started to feel the effects of deflation caused by cheap "made-in-China" products. Great quantities of low-priced goods produced in China with its cheap labor costs were imported into Japan, causing the trend in falling prices to get worse.

The Japanese economy was caught in a deflationary spiral, a vicious circle of falling corporate profits, falling capital investment, falling employment, falling wages, and stagnant consumption.

Government Deficits *(See Fig. 4-1)*

After the bubble's collapse, the Japanese economy went into long-term stagnation. There was a fall in corporate profits and a decline in tax revenues. In addition, Japan's budget balance worsened significantly as a result of repeated government fiscal stimulus packages designed to bring the economy back to life. Japan now has the largest budget deficit among developed economies.

Numerous economic indicators underline the seriousness of the government's fiscal deficit.

Government bond issuance is rising. Japanese government debt is expected to hit 932 trillion yen at the end of fiscal 2020. This is the equivalent of 15 years' worth of tax receipts. In the fiscal 2020 budget, the ratio of dependence on government bonds rose to 31.7%. Interest payments and government bond redemption accounts for nearly 20% of the general account.

When the debts of regional authorities are factored in, total public sector debt rises to 1,125 trillion yen. One statistic often used in international comparisons is government debt (of central and local governments) expressed as a ratio of GDP. At the fiscal 2020 year-end, Japan's ratio is expected to be somewhere in excess of 200%, overwhelmingly the highest level among developed nations.

The government has finally recognized it has to deal with the worsening budget deficit. It is now moving ahead with fiscal reforms, such as the current "triple reform." The goal of the triple reform is to transfer tax sources from the central government to the local level and reduce subsidies and tax grants from the central government. The government is also trying to revitalize the economy through measures such as deregulation and structural reform, because a revitalized economy means increased tax revenues.

Reform of the Financial System

After the war, the Japanese financial system developed under the guidance of the powerful Ministry of Finance. In order to nurture and protect all financial institutions, the Ministry introduced regulations designed to make sure that even the weakest banks would survive. This policy was called the "convoy system." Decades later, when other countries around the world began implementing financial reforms, Japan fell behind. These countries liberalized interest rates and financial products and removed barriers between the banking, stockbroking, and insurance industries. The Japanese financial system started to lose international competitiveness.

In 1996, Prime Minister Ryutaro Hashimoto announced a reform of the financial system. The reform was modeled on the "Big Bang" financial reforms in the United Kingdom and aimed at fostering freedom, fairness, and internationalization. It was called the "Japanese Big Bang." In the end, the Big

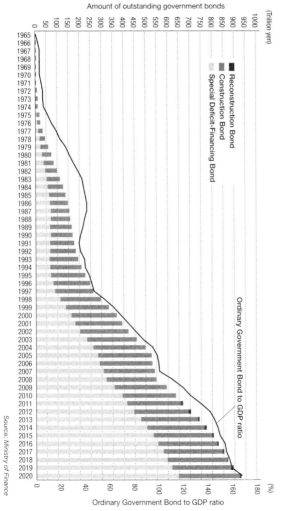

Fig. 4-1 Changes in Outstanding Government Bonds

Source: Ministry of Finance

Bang in Japan failed and only ended up eating away at the strength of Japanese banks (already weakened by non-performing loans after the collapse of the bubble) and caused more problems for the financial system.

In the mid-1990s a series of Japanese financial institutions went bankrupt. After this, credit risk and liquidity risk in overseas markets rose for Japanese banks. Major foreign banks were no longer willing to lend Japanese banks money and Japanese banks had to pay a premium above the normal interest rate to borrow money from foreign banks. This premium was called the "Japan premium." The creditworthiness of Japanese banks was restored when the government injected public money into the major banks. As a result, the "Japan premium" was dropped.

In 2005, when the disposal of non-performing loans was almost complete and the financial system stabilized, the temporary suspension of the ceiling on insured deposits was removed. Now depositors must choose their banks more carefully by examining a bank's financial situation and the financial products they offer.

Deregulation

Japan has placed many restrictions and regulations on many sectors, such as finance, retail sales, communications, and construction. Foreign countries are very critical of these regulations and restrictions. In recent years, in response to this criticism, Japan has steadily removed these regulations and restrictions. This is a part of the structural reform movement.

From the late 1970s, particularly in the United States and the United Kingdom, reforms were enacted toward "smaller government" and greater dependence on free market mechanisms.

Japan started privatization and deregulation only in the 1980s. In addition to privatizing Japan National Railways, Nippon Telegraph and Telephone Public Corporation, and the Japan Tobacco and Salt Public Corporation, regulations were relaxed for the finance and air-travel sectors. But progress was slow.

In the 1990s, there was discussion about deregulating the logistics, electric-power generation, gas, and communications sectors. Regulations governing market participation, charges, and business operations were criticized as "non-tariff barriers" in the U.S.-Japan Structural Impediments Initiative and other forums.

Other kinds of deregulation are still being examined and implemented in various sectors. Regulations obstruct technological innovation, artificially preserve companies and industries with low productivity, and reduce efficiency. However, industries where regulations are removed or relaxed face tough competition under the free market.

Corporate Restructuring

In the economic stagnation that followed the collapse of the bubble, Japanese corporations suffered from excess capacity, excess employment, and excessive debt. To solve these problems, many companies undertook bold corporate restructuring and reorganized their businesses, cut staff, and sold off assets.

Lifetime employment had been the standard practice at Japanese companies. Suddenly, cutting staff—something that seldom happened in the past—became a common practice. In some cases staff numbers were allowed to fall naturally by freezing the hiring of new university graduates or by getting people to volunteer for early retirement. Personnel cuts were often directed at workers who were middle-aged or above and had relatively high salaries. Frequently employees were put into a position where they felt they had no choice but to leave, such as being transferred to sections where they had no experience or to subsidiary companies.

These personnel cuts were effective in cutting costs, but they also created new problems. In the days when workers took lifetime employment for granted, they had a sense of security. This security made it possible for employees to devote themselves to their work. Loyalty and company spirit were the engines that drove Japanese corporations and the Japanese economy.

However, when companies decided to abandon the lifetime employment system and start cutting staff, the trust between company and employee broke down. Employee loyalty and company spirit suffered. Pay structures based on ability and performance are now being introduced, making employees weaker team players and encouraging them to take only jobs that produce quick results.

Japanese companies will soon have to reexamine

their personnel systems and the sort of relationships they build with their employees if they want to achieve the best results.

A More Flexible Labor Market *(See Fig. 4-2)*

The personnel system based upon lifetime employment and the seniority system were a unique feature of Japanese-style management. This system is now being taken apart. Performance-based pay is being introduced, and the number of people changing or quitting their jobs is on the increase. Also, companies that don't want to hire permanent full-time employees at high salaries are using employment agency staff, part-time employees, and "temps" (temporary employees) instead. As a result, the labor market has become more liquid.

Often people trying to get their first job or to change jobs cannot meet the skill, ability, salary, or age criteria set by the employer. This results in a "mismatch" between jobs and jobseekers. Therefore, even if the economy recovers and job vacancies increase, the total number of jobs filled might not grow.

In order to make effective use of human resources and to increase the productivity and competitiveness of the Japanese economy, Japan must solve this problem. In other words, Japan must create a society that encourages workers to move into new and growing industries.

Fig. 4-2 Number of Full-time Employees, Part-time Employees, and Percentage of Part-time Employees of Total Employment

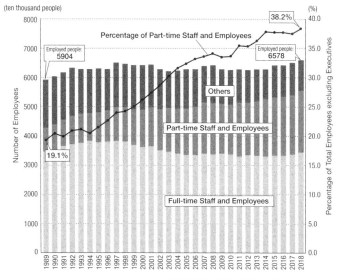

Source: *Ministry of Internal Affairs and Communications*

How to improve job matching is a hot topic. In the future, job placement services and careful job counseling will be needed for people looking for their first job or changing jobs. It will also be important to

The Changing Attitude Toward Work

After the corporate sector started to cut back on full-time employment in the late 1990s, resulting in a more flexible labor market, young Japanese people's attitude to work changed significantly.

One sign of this was the rapid increase in so-called freeters. The word is a combination of the English "free" and the German "arbeiter" (part-time worker). In Japanese, a freeter means someone who does not aspire to have a full-time job at a company. Instead, they prefer to work as part-timers or temp staffers. Freeters enjoy a high degree of autonomy as regards their working hours and their ability to pursue their own interests. At times when the economy is stagnant and it is hard for young people to find a job, the number of freeters tends to rise. Some people point to their increase as something that could destabilize the traditional structures of Japanese society.

Another group of young people known as NEETs

provide suitable professional training. This training should be based on the latest human-resources needs of companies.

---

also appeared. NEETs are dropouts, people with few touchpoints to society, or people who have lost confidence and given up as a result of failing to find work. Just like freeters, the number of NEETs is also on the rise. Some people become *hikikomori* (socially isolated), not going to work or to school, having nothing to do with anyone outside their immediate family and never leaving home. The problem is not limited to younger people and recently NEETs and *hikikomori* of an advanced age are becoming a social problem.

Since NEETs and *hikikomori* have no interest in working or participating in the labor market, any increase in their number will hinder Japanese economic growth. Seen in fiscal terms, the fact that many young people who should be paying into social security are instead receiving welfare benefits causes an outflow of government funds. Schools, business and society at large must unite to solve this problem.

The Aging Society and Declining Birth Rate
(See Fig. 4-3)

The problems of the aging society and declining birth rate are shaking the Japanese economy to its roots.

The number of births in Japan has been on the decline since 1973, and the present level is just half of what it was then. The birthrate, which was at a high of an average 2.16 children per woman in 1971, is also in continuous decline, registering a low of 1.26 children per woman in 2005.

On the other hand, the proportion of elderly people (defined as people over 65) in the population stood at 28.7% in 2020. This ratio is predicted to rise to 33.3% (meaning one out of every three people will be old) by 2036, and to 38.4% by 2065. This is the aging society in action. Japan's switch to an aging society with a declining birth rate is taking place at unprecedented speed.

Japan's overall population peaked at 128.08 million people in 2008 before entering a downward trend which is expected to continue for the long term. Forecasts have the population crashing through 100 million in 2053 and dropping to 88.08

million in 2065. Since this population decline will be focused on the young and middle-aged cohorts who are the most active consumers, there are concerns that it will lead to a slowdown in consumption and a fall in domestic demand. Meanwhile, the decline in the working-age population (people from 15 to 64 years old) is a particularly serious problem. Having

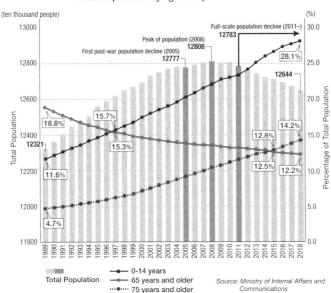

Fig. 4-3 Changes in Total Population and Percentage of Total Population by Age Group

peaked at 87.17 million in 1995, this too is on the way down. The working-age population is forecast to fall through the 70 million mark to 69.51 million in 2029, before falling to 45.29 million in 2065. There are worries that this decline in the working-age population will deplete the strength of the corporate sector and lead to economic deceleration.

As the cost of social security programs like pensions, nursing, and health care rise, the burden on individual citizens will increase. Thus, reform of the social security system is a matter of great urgency.

Environmental Problems

Since the 1990s, environmental problems such as global warming and the destruction of the ozone layer have come to the fore as worldwide challenges that all countries need to work together to address. Companies are under pressure to acknowledge the necessity of preserving the environment and reducing the environmental burden.

There are many different ways of responding to environmental issues. These include using natural resources and energy efficiently, reducing emissions of CO_2 and other "greenhouse gases," reducing waste, restricting the use of toxic chemicals, developing environmental technology, and marketing environment-friendly products.

The Kyoto Protocol was signed in 2005 in a bid to reduce greenhouse gas emissions. It set targets for advanced nations to reduce emissions.

In 2015, the Paris Agreement was established as the successor to the Kyoto Protocol as a new international framework for 2020 onward. The Paris Agreement came into force in 2016. The Paris Agreement sets common long-term global targets. The goal is to try to limit average global temperature rise to well below 2 degrees and ideally to 1.5 degrees Celsius relative to pre-industrial levels. The Paris Agreement is a framework which demands reductions in greenhouse gas emissions by all signatory countries, including developing countries. Japan has set itself a goal of cutting its 2030 emissions by 26% vis-à-vis 2013 levels.

Coping with environmental issues is not only about the negative impact of heavy financial burdens. There is a positive side, as well. Environmental problems can provide companies with new opportunities for growth in developing environmental technology.

For example, Japanese manufacturers like Honda and Toyota Motor are pioneering the development and marketing of fuel-cell hybrid vehicles. As environmental consciousness grows worldwide, clean and energy-efficient fuel-cell hybrid vehicles are expected to become mainstream. With this new technology, Japanese carmakers are likely to keep their leading role in the global car industry well into the future.

Japanese companies can maintain and increase their competitiveness by developing and marketing advanced environmental technology before other companies or countries do. Dealing with environmental problems appropriately could be a major factor in Japan's economic recovery.

PART FIVE

The Japanese Economy in the 21st Century

読みはじめる前に

目を通しておくと、この章が読みやすくなる経済用語です。

Abenomics	アベノミクス
Act on Promotion of Women's Participation and Advancement in the Workplace	女性活躍推進法
declare a state of emergency	緊急事態宣言を発令する
disposable income	可処分所得
dynamic engagement of all citizens	一億総活躍
excessive inflow	転入超過
Gini coefficient	ジニ係数
Great East Japan Earthquake	東日本大震災
inbound tourists	訪日外国人旅行客（インバウンド）
Industrial Revitalization Corporation of Japan	産業再生機構
inflation target	インフレターゲット，インフレ目標
Izanami Boom	いざなみ景気
Japan Tourism Agency（JTA）	観光庁
Lehman shock（The 2008 Financial Crisis）	リーマン・ショック
management position	管理職
Ministry of Land, Infrastructure, Transport and Tourism	国土交通省
mood of self-restraint	自粛ムード
new normal	ニューノーマル，新しい生活様式
novel coronavirus（Covid-19）	新型コロナウイルス

overconcentration in Tokyo	東京一極集中
paid-in capital	資本金，払込資本
privatization	民営化
privatize the post office	郵政を民営化する
quantitative and qualitative financial easing	量的・質的金融緩和
regional revitalization	地方創生
relative income poverty	相対的貧困
rolling blackout	計画停電，輪番停電
single-parent household	ひとり親世帯
special zones for structural reform	構造改革特区
stay-at-home mother	専業主婦
structural reform	構造改革
subprime loan	サブプライムローン
supply chain	サプライチェーン
telework	テレワーク
three arrows	(アベノミクス) 3 本の矢。bold monetary policy (大胆な金融政策)，flexible fiscal policy (機動的な財政政策)，growth strategy designed to stimulate private-sector investment (民間投資を喚起する成長戦略)
unemployment rate	失業率 (完全失業率)
unequal society	格差社会
unfair termination	雇い止め
wealth gap	貧富の差
work style reform	働き方改革

Structural Reform

After the collapse of the bubble, Japan was unable to get out of its long economic slump. By the end of the 1990s, Japan's economy and society seemed to have reached a dead end. This was the situation when Prime Minister Junichiro Koizumi came on the scene in April 2001. His slogan was "without reform, there can be no economic growth."

Prime Minister Koizumi argued that it was necessary to implement "structural reforms" to spur economic growth and maintain expansion. These reforms would remove inefficiencies from the economy and produce a socio-economic system suitable for the 21st century.

Put in simple terms, "structural reform" means creating a framework in which new growth industries and products replace stagnating industries and products. This sort of "creative destruction" is regarded as the source of all economic growth. It makes economic resources like labor and capital shift from inefficient industrial sectors to efficient, growing sectors.

The Koizumi administration's structural reform

policy had two basic philosophies: (1) "Let the private sector do what the private sector does best," and (2) "Let local governments do what local governments do best." Koizumi pushed ahead with reforms in seven areas: (1) privatization and deregulation, (2) support for new ventures, (3) the reform of the social security system, (4) human resources training and scientific and technological innovation, (5) the renovation of people's lives, (6) the independence and revitalization of local regions and their governments, and (7) the reform of government finances.

The government has begun implementing "special zones for structural reform." These zones are exempt from normal regulations in recognition of an area's special character. These special zones are being rolled out in small steps on a national basis.

The Koizumi administration steamrollered all opposition to privatize the post office, something that was seen as the Holy Grail of structural reform. It also went ahead with the privatization of the Highway Public Corporation, Teito Rapid Transit Authority (now called Tokyo Metro), and government financial institutions.

In 2003, the Koizumi administration set up the

Industrial Revitalization Corporation of Japan which spearheaded the restructuring of Daiei (supermarkets) and Kanebo (cosmetics), both companies which were mired in debt despite having high-quality management.

It also pushed ahead vigorously with the disposal of financial institutions' non-performing loans which had been weighing on the economy since the collapse of the bubble economy. After peaking in the March quarter of 2002, the balance of non-performing loans started to decline steadily.

The Nikkei Average fell to what was then a post-bubble low of 7,608 in April 2003, but subsequently started to rise. Between February 2002 and February 2008, the economy went through a 73-month-long expansionary phase known as the Izanami Boom. The growth rate, however, was so subdued that no one felt any richer.

The 2008 Financial Crisis

From the summer of 2007, it started to become clear that more and more subprime loans (home loans structured to enable people on low incomes to buy a house) were being defaulted on in the United States. As the repayment of these subprime loans fell ever more into arrears, Lehman Brothers, one of the biggest American investment banks, filed for bankruptcy in September 2008 after suffering a huge loss.

The impact of what in Japanese is referred to as the "Lehman shock" was not restricted to the United States, but rippled across the world. Stock indices nosedived, while fears about creditworthiness plunged financial markets into a state of paralysis. Both consumption and investment collapsed and the world fell into a "once-in-a-100-year recession."

Japan suffered very severe impacts. The Nikkei Average—which had been at 12,214 just before Lehman Brothers' collapse—fell through the 7,000-yen mark just one month later. Exports to the United States, particularly in the automobile sector, fell by 60%. Overall exports were halved. National champions like Toyota Motor and Hitachi posted losses.

The employment situation also took a turn for the worse. In late 2008, unfair termination (in which irregular employment contracts are not renewed) and *haken-giri* (downsizing by laying off temp workers) both became serious social problems. By July

2009, the unemployment rate had risen to 5.5%. The growth rate of actual GDP was minus 3.4% for fiscal 2008 and minus 2.2% for fiscal 2009, making for two consecutive years of negative growth.

The Great East Japan Earthquake

When the sharp economic slump that followed the collapse of Lehman Brothers was finally showing some signs of recovery, trouble struck the Japanese economy for a second time. The Great East Japan Earthquake occurred on March 3, 2011.

A huge earthquake with a maximum seismic intensity of 7 on the Japanese scale (magnitude 9), followed by a gigantic tsunami, hit the Tohoku region, causing serious harm to both people and buildings in eastern Japan. The earthquake caused an accident at the Fukushima Daiichi nuclear power plant of Tokyo Electric Power Company (TEPCO). Due to concerns about its ability to provide electricity, TEPCO initiated rolling blackouts in the areas it supplied, switching off the power region by region in a pre-planned order.

The Tohoku region, which suffered the greatest

damage from the earthquake, was home to a cluster of factories making components and materials. Not only did the damaged factories cease operations; even in areas which had not been directly impacted, breaks in the supply chain made it difficult to procure materials and components. Factory production slowed or came to a complete halt over a wide area.

A falling-off in consumer animal spirits and a mood of self-restraint led to a major fall in personal consumption centered around services like travel, bars and restaurants, as well as luxury goods. The earthquake inflicted a heavy blow, pushing the Japanese economy back into a slump.

Abenomics

The disorder caused by the Great East Japan Earthquake was still ongoing in 2012 when the Liberal Democratic Party (LDP) took back power from the Democratic Party of Japan. Shinzo Abe, who had stepped down as prime minister in 2007, resumed the premiership and the second Abe cabinet got underway.

The new prime minister announced an economic

policy, colloquially known as Abenomics, designed to break free of deflation. He planned to revive the Japanese economy through the "three arrows" of bold monetary policy, flexible fiscal policy, and a growth strategy designed to stimulate private-sector investment.

When Haruhiko Kuroda took over the reins at the Bank of Japan in March 2013, he embarked on a bold policy of quantitative and qualitative financial easing. The value of the yen plummeted, with the exchange rate, which had stood at 80 or so yen to the dollar at the end of 2012, falling to the 120-yen range. Increased weakness in the yen led to a marked improvement in business performance, particularly in the manufacturing sector. The Nikkei Average, which had been hovering around the 10,000-yen mark, shot up into the 15,000s within five months of Abe taking office, and hit a high of 24,270 in 2018. The upturn that had started with the advent of the second Abe administration lasted until October 2018, a period of 71 months, making it the second longest expansion in the whole postwar period.

The policies of the Abe administration delivered undeniable results in terms of reviving the Japanese economy after the body blows it had suffered in the 2008 financial crisis and the Great East Japan Earthquake. Abe's team looked for ways to reform Japan's social and economic systems under slogans like "regional revitalization," "the dynamic engagement of all citizens," and "work style reform."

One thing the administration could not do was to achieve the inflation target of 2% in two years that it had set itself. Nor did the growth strategy deliver any very tangible benefits. The main result of Abe's aggressive fiscal policy was a rise in the debt of the national and local governments from 932 trillion yen at the March end of the fiscal year in 2012 to over 1,122 trillion yen at the March end of the fiscal year in 2020.

Inbound Tourism *(See Fig. 5-1)*

One of the government's economic revitalization policies involved an effort to increase the number of foreign visitors, or inbound tourists, coming to Japan. The aim was to get consumption by foreign visitors to compensate for the decline in domestic consumption caused by the aging population and falling birthrate.

The government started to take steps in 2003 with the aim of increasing the annual number of foreign visitors to Japan, which was then stagnant at around the 5 million mark, in order to make a Japan a "tourism superpower." The Ministry of Land, Infrastructure, Transport and Tourism led the charge with the launch of the "Visit JAPAN" campaign. It teamed up with overseas media outlets and travel agencies to promote the attractions of Japanese culture and travel.

Fig. 5-1 Changes in the Number of Foreign Visitors to Japan and Travel Consumption

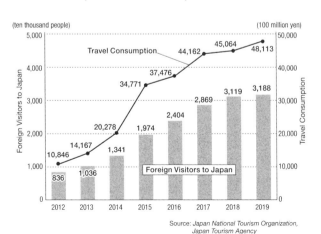

Source: *Japan National Tourism Organization, Japan Tourism Agency*

The Japan Tourism Agency (JTA) was created in 2008 as an affiliated agency of the Ministry of Land, Infrastructure, Transport and Tourism. The JTA launched aggressive policies to boost inbound tourist numbers. It supported the creation of tourist destinations with a high level of international competitiveness and ran promotions for specific regions. It also sought to attract international conferences and overseas businesses for training to Japan. Starting in 2013, it loosened visa regulations for certain countries, many of them in Asia.

These steps proved effective and visitor numbers broke through the 10 million mark in 2013. They continued to rise, hitting 31.88 million in 2019. With the increase in overseas arrivals, tourism expenditure also rose, exceeding 4.8 trillion yen in 2019. When the economic ripple effects (trade in commodities like agricultural products and fisheries) are added in, you can multiply that figure by 1.75, for a total of 7.8 trillion yen. Clearly, the impact that overseas visitors have on the Japanese economy has become very significant.

Overconcentration in Tokyo

One of the challenges the Japanese economy faces is the need to correct overconcentration in Tokyo and the capital region. The population of Tokyo increased by two million in the last 20 years to surpass 14 million people in 2020. While the population of Japan as a whole is falling, the concentration of people in Tokyo continues to rise, exacerbating the depopulation and decline of the regions.

Overconcentration increases the dangers posed by natural disasters. Half of companies with paid-in capital of over 100 million yen are headquartered in Tokyo. Tokyo is also home to over half the headquarters of listed companies. With the key functions of the country concentrated in Tokyo, there is the very real possibility that a major disaster, like an earthquake or catastrophic rainfall, could provoke dysfunction in the Japanese economy.

The Abe administration tried to promote regional revitalization and correct overconcentration in Tokyo. It established the post of minister of state for the promotion of overcoming population decline and vitalizing the local economy in Japan. It also strove to transfer government functions to the regions, successfully shifting the Agency for Cultural Affairs to Kyoto and a part of the Consumer Affairs Agency to Hiroshima. It also encouraged elderly people to move out to the regions.

Nonetheless, excessive inflows into the Tokyo region continue unchecked, with more people migrating in than people migrating out. Greater efforts, from dispersing the functions of the capital around the country to telework, are needed to halt the decline of the regions and to help smaller towns and cities develop.

The Growth of Inequality

Japan endured a long recession after the collapse of the bubble economy. This led to a widening of the wealth gap and the advent of an unequal society.

The standard indicator used to measure income inequality is known as the Gini coefficient. Expressed by a number between zero and one, the closer the number is to one, the greater the inequality. Research conducted in 2017 by the Ministry of Health, Labor and Welfare found that Japan had a Gini coefficient of 0.559. It had slowly risen from a level of around 0.4 in the latter half of the 1980s, surpassing 0.5 in 2005.

Relative income poverty is another similar indicator. This refers to people who are poor relative to the prevalent cultural and lifestyle level of a particular country. Specifically, it refers to people with household disposable income below 50% of the national median. According to OECD research, Japan's relative income poverty rate has hovered around 16% in recent years, giving it the second-highest level among the major economies after the United States. One Japanese person out of six is living in relative income poverty.

Changes in the industrial structure, a rise in irregular employment, an increasingly elderly population as a result of the declining birthrate and aging, and the increase in single-parent households are all cited as reasons for the rise in relative income poverty.

Income disparity is linked to disparity in education. Children who are born and brought up in low-income households cannot secure an adequate education, as they are often unable to proceed to further education or to get the opportunity for extra-curricular study. This limits their job options and has a negative influence on their future earning potential. It is possible that poverty and the disparities it creates can end up extending across several generations.

Widening inequality can lead to social and political instability and hinder economic growth. Suitable policies to rectify the situation need to be introduced as a matter of urgency.

A Society with the Active Participation of Women *(See Fig. 5-2)*

In Japan, both the overall population and the working-age population are in decline. If the country wants to secure a sufficient supply of labor and keep the economy strong, it needs to provide opportunities for women and older people who want to work to do so.

In the postwar period, the accepted social model involved men working while women took care of the family as full-time homemakers. The old values that men should go out to work while women handle housework and child-rearing have changed. In the second half of the 1990s, the number of households in which both husband and wife were working exceeded the number of households with stay-at-home mothers.

The government is implementing policies to create a society in which women can be active participants, putting their individuality and their abilities to good use. The Act on Promotion of Women's Participation and Advancement in the Workplace was passed in 2016. This made employers (central government, local authorities and private-sector companies)

Fig. 5-2 Changes in Percentage of Women in Management Positions by Rank in the Private Sector

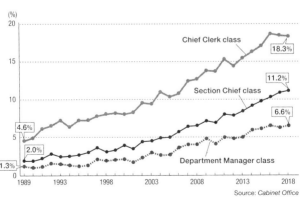

Source: *Cabinet Office*

assess the level of female participation and activity in their organizations, itemize the challenges women face, establish numerical targets and formulate and publish action plans.

To assess the level of female activity, organizations need to figure out the ratio of female hires; the difference in length of service between males and females; working hours; and the percentage of women in management positions.

The jewel in the crown of the government's efforts to empower women was the goal it set for women to fill 30% of leadership positions in every field of society. They originally designated 2020 as the year to achieve this goal. Since, however, the proportion of women in management position in both the public and private sectors still remains low, the goal has been pushed down the road to "as early as possible in the 2020s." A new target of achieving an equal ratio of men and women in management positions in the 2030s has been set as part of the aim of creating a society in which women participate more actively.

The Ravages of Covid-19

Having originated in Hubei Province in China, the novel coronavirus went on to infect people worldwide in 2020. Countries everywhere were desperate to contain the disease. They blocked off cities, imposed lockdowns on people, and restricted or closed bars, restaurants, shops and factories. The pandemic brought activity to a standstill and the global economy quickly fell into a slump.

The Japanese economy suffered a tremendous negative impact. With infections soaring, the government declared a state of emergency in April 2020. With shops selling essential goods as the sole exception, the government requested shops to temporarily shut down and events to be cancelled or postponed, while also asking people to stay at home unless they had an urgent reason not to do so. Companies introduced telework and working from home grew rapidly and on a large scale.

Although the state of emergency was lifted in May, the negative impact of the pandemic continued to be felt in many areas. Personal consumption declined as people stopped eating out and travelling. The slump in the global economy led to the export of automobiles stagnating. Consumption by foreign visitors, which had expanded as a result of the drive to promote inbound tourism, was almost totally wiped out. Real GDP experienced its largest decline since World War II, exceeding even the financial crisis of 2008.

There are more and more households where jobs have been lost or incomes have declined as a result of the fallout from Covid-19. The campaigns the government launched to boost demand for domestic tourism and for bars and restaurants appear to be having limited impact. Many people, particularly older people, are choosing to stay indoors and avoid meeting in large groups for eating and drinking. Many companies are declaring bankruptcy. The slump in the Japanese economy is forecast to last a long time.

It is thought that there will be intermittent surges of coronavirus infections going forward. We need to learn to live with corona. That means figuring out the shape of the new normal, where economic and social life goes on even as the number of infections is held down.

Word List

A

□ **abandon** 名 ①自暴自棄 ②気まま、奔放 動 ①捨てる、放棄する ②（計画などを）中止する、断念する

□ **Abenomics** 名 アベノミクス《安倍晋三が第2次安倍内閣において掲げた、一連の経済政策に対して与えられた通称。主唱者である「安倍」の姓と、「エコノミクス（英：economics）」とを合わせた造語》

□ **ability** 名 ①できること、（～する）能力 ②才能

□ **abroad** 熟 from abroad 海外から

□ **accept** 動 ①受け入れる ②同意する、認める

□ **accident** 名 ①（不慮の）事故、災難 ②偶然

□ **acclaim** 動 ほめる、（拍手）かっさいを送る 名 賞賛、かっさい

□ **accord** 名 調和、一致 動 ①与える ②調和する、一致する

□ **according** 副《 – to ～》～によれば［よると］

□ **account** 名 ①計算書 ②勘定、預金口座 ③説明、報告、記述 general account 一般会計 動 ①《 – for ～》～を説明する、～（の割合）を占める、～の原因となる ②～を…とみなす

account for ～の割合を占める、～を構成する

□ **accounting sheet** 会計帳簿、貸借対照表

□ **achieve** 動 成し遂げる、達成する、成功を収める

□ **acknowledge** 動（～として、～を）認める

■ **Act on Promotion of Women's Participation and Advancement in the Workplace** 女性活躍推進法

□ **active** 形 ①活動的な ②積極的な ③活動［作動］中の

□ **actively** 副 活発に、活動的に

□ **activity** 名 活動、活気

□ **actual** 形 実際の、現実の

□ **actually** 副 実際に、本当に、実は

□ **add** 動 ①加える、足す ②足し算をする ③言い添える

□ **addition** 名 ①付加、追加、添加 ②足し算 in addition 加えて、さらに in addition to ～に加えて、さらに

□ **address** 名 ①住所、アドレス ②演説 動 ①あて名を書く ②演説をする、話しかける

□ **adequate** 形 十分な、ふさわしい、

WORD LIST

適切な

□ **administration** 名 管理, 統治, 政権

□ **administrative** 形 ①行政の ②管理の, 運営［経営］上の

□ **administrative guidance** 行政指導

□ **adopt** 動 ①採択する, 選ぶ ②承認する ③養子にする

□ **advanced** 動 advance（進む）の過去, 過去分詞 形 上級の, 先に進んだ, 高等の

□ **advanced nation** 先進国

□ **advancement** 名 進歩, 前進, 昇進

□ **advantage** 名 有利な点［立場］, 強み, 優越

□ **advent** 名 ①《the –》到来, 出現 ②《A-》キリストの降臨, 降臨節

□ **affair** 名 ①事柄, 事件 ②《-s》業務, 仕事, やるべきこと

□ **affiliated agency** 外局

□ **age criteria** 年齢基準［制限］

□ **age group** 年齢層

□ **agency** 名 ①代理店, 仲介 ②機関, 政府機関 ③媒介, 媒体

□ **Agency for Cultural Affairs** 文化庁

□ **aggressive** 形 ①攻撃的な, 好戦的な ②活動的な ③強引な

□ **aging** 名 ①老化, 高齢化 ②熟成 ③時効 形 ①年老いた ②老朽化した ③熟成した

□ **aging society** 高齢化社会

□ **agreement** 名 ①合意, 協定 ②一致

□ **agricultural** 形 農業の, 農事の

□ **agricultural and land reform** 農地改革

□ **ahead** 熟 go ahead 進んで行う, 思い切って～する

□ **aim** 動 ①（武器・カメラなどを）向ける ②ねらう, 目指す 名 ねらい, 目標 with the aim of ～を目的として, ～のために

□ **air conditioner** エアコン, クーラー

□ **air raid** 空襲

□ **air-travel sector** 航空分野

□ **all** 熟 last of all 最後に

□ **Allied Occupation Army** 進駐軍, 占領軍（GHQ）

□ **allow** 動 ①許す,《– … to ～》…が～するのを可能にする, …に～させておく ②与える

□ **although** 接 ～だけれども, ～にもかかわらず, たとえ～でも

□ **American** 形 アメリカ（人）の

□ **amount** 名 ①量, 額 ②《the –》合計 額（総計～に）なる

□ **analyze** 動 ①分析する, 解析する, 細かく検討する ②精神分析する ③解剖する

□ **and so** そこで, それだから, それで

□ **animal spirits** 元気, 精気

□ **animated** 動 animate（生気を与える）の過去, 過去分詞 形 ①活気に満ちた ②アニメの

□ **anime** 名 アニメ

□ **annihilate** 動 滅ぼす, 壊滅させる, 絶滅させる

□ **announce** 動 （人に）知らせる, 公表する

□ **annual** 形 年1回の, 例年の, 年次の 名 ①年報 ②一年生植物

□ **annually** 副 毎年, 年1回

□ **anyone** 代 ①《疑問文・条件節で》誰か ②《否定文で》誰も（～ない）③《肯定文で》誰でも

□ **apart** 副 ①ばらばらに, 離れて ②別にして, それだけで come apart バラバラになる

□ **appear** 動 ①現れる, 見えてく

93

る ②(〜のように)見える, 〜らしい
appear to するように見える

□ **appliance** 名器具, 道具, (家庭用)電気製品

□ **appreciate** 動①正しく評価する, よさがわかる ②価値[相場]が上がる ③ありがたく思う

□ **appreciation** 名①正しい評価, 真価を認めること ②感謝

□ **approach** 動①接近する ②話を持ちかける 名接近, (〜へ)近づく道

□ **appropriately** 副ふさわしく, 適切なやり方で

□ **arbeiter** 名アルバイトをする人。ドイツ語で「労働者」の意。

□ **argue** 動①論じる, 議論する ②主張する

□ **army** 名軍隊, 《the –》陸軍

□ **arrear** 名①〔義務・約束の履行の〕遅れ, 滞り ②滞納(金), 未払い金

□ **arrival** 名①到着 ②到達

□ **arrow** 名矢, 矢のようなもの

□ **artificially** 副人為的に, 人工的に, 見かけ上は

□ **as a result** その結果(として)

□ **as a result of** 〜の結果(として)

□ **as a whole** 全体として

□ **as if** あたかも〜のように, まるで〜みたいに

□ **as well** なお, その上, 同様に

□ **as well as** 〜と同様に

□ **as 〜 as possible** できるだけ〜

□ **ASEAN** 略東南アジア諸国連合 (= Association of Southeast Asian Nations)

□ **Asia** 名アジア

□ **Asian Financial Crisis** アジア通貨危機

□ **aspire** 動熱望する, 切望する

□ **assemble** 動①集める, 集まる ②組み立てる

□ **assess** 動評価する, 査定する

□ **asset** 名財産, 資産, 価値のあるもの

□ **asset deflation** 資産デフレ

□ **at first** 最初は, 初めのうちは

□ **at home** 自宅で, 在宅して, 自国で

□ **at large** 全体として, 広く

□ **at one time** ある時には, かつては

□ **at present** 今のところ, 現在は, 目下

□ **at the end of** 〜の終わりに

□ **at the request of** 〜の要請により, 〜の要求に応じて

□ **attack** 動①襲う, 攻める ②非難する ③(病気が)おかす 名①攻撃, 非難 ②発作, 発病

□ **attempt** 動試みる, 企てる 名試み, 企て, 努力

□ **attention** 名①注意, 集中 ②配慮, 手当て, 世話 間《号令として》気をつけ

□ **attitude** 名姿勢, 態度, 心構え

□ **attract** 動①引きつける, 引く ②魅力がある, 魅了する

□ **attraction** 名引きつけるもの, 出し物, アトラクション

□ **audio-visual** 名オーディオビジュアル, AV, 視聴覚 形視聴覚の

□ **Australia** 名オーストラリア《国名》

□ **authority** 名①権威, 権力, 権限 ②《the -ties》(関係)当局

□ **auto industry** 自動車産業

□ **automobile** 名自動車

□ **automobile-related** 形自動車関連の

□ **automotive** 形自動車の, 自力推進の

□ **autonomy** 名自律(性), 自主(性)

□ **average** 名平均(値), 並み on (the) average 平均して 形平均の, 普通の 動平均して～になる

□ **avoid** 動避ける, (～を) しないようにする

□ **away** 熟 stay away from ～から離れている

B

□ **bad loan** 不良債権

□ **bakugai** 名爆買い《一度に大量にまとめ買いすることを表す語。主に来日した中国人観光客が大量に商品を購買する行為を指す》

□ **balance** 名①均衡, 平均, 落ち着き ②てんびん ③残高, 差額 動釣り合いをとる

□ **Bank of Japan (BOJ)** 日本銀行, 日銀

□ **banking** 動bank (取引する) の現在分詞 名銀行業

□ **bankrupt** 名破産(者) 形破産した, 支払い能力のない go bankrupt 倒産する

□ **bankruptcy** 名破産, 倒産

□ **bar** 名①酒場 ②棒, かんぬき ③障害 (物) 動かんぬきで閉める

□ **barrier** 名さく, 防壁, 障害(物), 障壁 動防壁で囲む

□ **base** 名基礎, 土台, 本部 動《 – on ～》～に基礎を置く, 基づく

□ **basic** 形基礎の, 基本の 名《-s》基礎, 基本, 必需品

□ **basic industry** 基幹産業

□ **basically** 副基本的には, 大筋では

□ **basis** 名①土台, 基礎 ②基準, 原理 ③根拠 ④主成分

□ **because of** ～のために, ～の理由で

□ **beef** 名牛肉

□ **beginning** 動begin (始まる) の現在分詞 名初め, 始まり

□ **behind** 前①～の後ろに, ～の背後に ②～に遅れて, ～に劣って lie behind ～の後方[背後]にある 副①後ろに, 背後に ②遅れて, 劣って fall behind 取り残される, 後れを取る

□ **being** 動be (～である) の現在分詞 名存在, 生命, 人間

□ **belief** 名信じること, 信念, 信用

□ **belong to** ～に属する

□ **belonging** 動belong (属する) の現在分詞 《-s》持ち物, 所有物, 財産

□ **below** 前①～より下に ②～以下の, ～より劣る 副下に[へ]

□ **benefit** 名①利益, 恩恵 ②(失業保険・年金などの) 手当, 給付(金) 動利益を得る, (～の) 役に立つ

□ **between A and B** AとBの間に

□ **bid** 動①(競売・入札などで) 値をつける, 入札する ②(トランプなどでせり札を) 宣言する 名①付け値, 入札 ②(トランプなどで) 宣言, ビッド

□ **Big Bang** 《the – 》〔金融市場の〕ビッグ・バン《1986年10月27日にイギリス証券取引所が行った大胆な規制自由化》

□ **birth** 名①出産, 誕生 ②生まれ, 起源, (よい) 家柄 give birth to ～を生む

□ **birth rate** 出生率

□ **birthrate** 名出生率

□ **blanket** 名毛布 動毛布でくるむ

□ **blow** 動①(風が) 吹く, (風が) ～を吹き飛ばす ②息を吹く, (鼻を) かむ ③破裂する ④吹奏する 名①(風の) ひと吹き, 突風 ②(楽器の) 吹奏 ③打撃

□ **board of directors** 取締役会

□ **bold** 形①勇敢な, 大胆な, 奔放な ②ずうずうしい ③派手な ④(文字が) 太字の

□ **bold monetary policy** 大胆な
金融政策

□ **bond** 名 ①縛るもの, ひも ②結び
つき, 結束 ③《-s》束縛 ④契約, 約定
⑤保証 (人・金), 担保 ⑥債券, 公債,
社債, 債務証書 ⑦接着, 接着剤 動 ①
担保に入れる, 債券に振り替える ②
保証人になる, 保証する ③接着する
[させる], 結合する

□ **boom** 名 ブーム, 急成長 動 急騰す
る

□ **boost** 動 ①後押し, 応援, 励まし
②値上げ 動 ①押し上げる ②後押し
する, 後援する ③ (値段を) つり上げ
る ④景気をあおる

□ **borrower** 名 借り手

□ **both A and B** A も B も

□ **break out** 発生する, 急に起こる,
(戦争が) 勃発する

□ **break through** ～を打ち破る

□ **break up** ばらばらになる, 解散さ
せる

□ **breakup** 名 崩壊, 解体, 解消

□ **brief** 形 ①短い時間の ②簡単な
名 要点, 概要

□ **bring about** 引き起こす

□ **bring back to life** 生き返る, 息
を吹き返す

□ **bring up** 育てる, 連れて行く

□ **broad** 形 ①幅の広い ②寛大な ③
明白な 副 すっかり, 十分に

□ **broadcast** 名 放送, 番組 動 放送
する, 広める 形 放送の

□ **broaden** 動 広がる, 広げる

□ **Brunei** 名 ブルネイ《国名》

□ **bubble** 名 泡 動 泡立つ, 沸き立つ

□ **Bubble Boom** バブル景気《1986
年 12 月～1991 年 2 月までの 51 ヵ月間
に起こった, 資産価格の上昇と好景
気》

□ **bubble economy** バブル経済

□ **budget** 名 ①経費 ②予算 動 予算

を立てる

□ **budget deficit** 財政赤字

□ **building** 名 build (建てる) の現在
分詞 名 建物, 建造物, ビルディング

□ **burden** 名 ①荷 ②重荷 動 荷 [負
担] を負わす

□ **bureaucrat** 名 役人, 官僚主義的
な人

C

□ **cabinet** 名 ①飾り棚 ②《C-》内閣,
閣僚

□ **Cabinet Office** 内閣府

□ **calculate** 動 ①計算する, 算出す
る ②見積もる, 予想する

□ **calculator** 名 計算機, 電卓

□ **campaign** 名 ①キャンペーン (活
動, 運動) ②政治運動, 選挙運動 ③
軍事行動 動 ①従軍する ②運動に参
加する

□ **Canada** 名 カナダ《国名》

□ **cancel** 動 ～をキャンセルする, ～
を取り消す, ～を中止する

□ **capacity** 名 ①定員, 容量 ②能力,
(潜在的な) 可能性

□ **capital** 名 ①首都 ②大文字 ③資
本 (金) 形 ①資本の ②首都の ③最
も重要な ④大文字の

□ **capital investment** 設備投資

□ **capital market** 資本市場

□ **capital trading practice** 資本
取引慣行

□ **care** 熟 health care 医療 take
care of ～の世話をする, ～面倒を見
る, ～を管理する

□ **carmaker** 名 自動車製造業者

□ **carry out** [計画を] 実行する

□ **cartoon** 名 時事風刺漫画, アニメ
映画

□ **category** 名 カテゴリー, 種類, 部

類

- [ ] **cease** 動やむ, やめる, 中止する 名終止

- [ ] **ceiling** 名①天井 ②上限, 最高価格

- [ ] **Celsius** 名〔温度計の〕セ氏(摂氏), セ氏温度計

- [ ] **central** 形中央の, 主要な

- [ ] **central bank governor** 中央銀行総裁

- [ ] **central government** 中央政府

- [ ] **certain** 形①確実な, 必ず~する ②(人が)確信した ③ある ④いくらかの 代(~の中の)いくつか

- [ ] **challenge** 名①挑戦 ②難関 動挑む, 試す

- [ ] **champion** 名優勝者, チャンピオン

- [ ] **chaos** 名無秩序, 混乱状態

- [ ] **character** 名①特性, 個性 ②(小説・劇などの)登場人物 ③文字, 記号 ④品性, 人格

- [ ] **charge** 動①(代金を)請求する ②(~を…に)負わせる ③命じる 名①請求金額, 料金 ②責任 ③非難, 告発

- [ ] **chemical products** 化学製品

- [ ] **chief clerk** 係長

- [ ] **chiefly** 副主として, まず第一に

- [ ] **child-rearing** 名子育て, 育児

- [ ] **Chile** 名チリ《国名》

- [ ] **China** 名①中国《国名》②《c-》陶磁器, 瀬戸物

- [ ] **Chinese** 形中国(人)の 名①中国人 ②中国語

- [ ] **choice** 名選択(の範囲・自由), えり好み, 選ばれた人［物］ **have no choice but to** ~するしかない 形精選した

- [ ] **circle** 名①円, 円周, 輪 ②循環, 軌道 ③仲間, サークル **vicious circle** 悪循環 動回る, 囲む

- [ ] **cite** 動言及する, 引用する 名言及,

引用

- [ ] **citizen** 名①市民, 国民 ②住民, 民間人

- [ ] **civilian** 名一般市民, 民間人 形民間の, 文民の

- [ ] **clear** 形①はっきりした, 明白な ②澄んだ ③(よく)晴れた 動①はっきりさせる ②片づける ③晴れる 副①はっきりと ②すっかり, 完全に

- [ ] **clearly** 副①明らかに, はっきりと ②《返答に用いて》そのとおり

- [ ] **client company** 取引先

- [ ] **closed** 動 close (閉まる)の過去, 過去分詞 形閉じた, 閉鎖した

- [ ] **closely** 副①密接に ②念入りに, 詳しく ③ぴったりと

- [ ] **clothing** 動 clothe (服を着せる)の現在分詞 名衣類, 衣料品

- [ ] **cluster** 名(花・実などの)房, (密集した動物の)群れ, 一団 動群がる

- [ ] **CO₂** 名二酸化炭素

- [ ] **coal** 名石炭, 木炭 動石炭を積み込む

- [ ] **code** 名①法典 ②規準, 慣例 ③コード, 番号 **tax code** 税法 動コード化する

- [ ] **coefficient** 名係数, 率

- [ ] **cohort** 名《統計》群, コ(ー)ホート

- [ ] **collaborate** 動協力する, 協力して働く

- [ ] **collapse** 名崩壊, 倒壊 動崩壊する, 崩れる, 失敗する

- [ ] **collateral** 名①担保(物件) ②付帯事実 ③直属でない親族 形①担保の, 見返りの ②付随的な ③直属でない親族の

- [ ] **colloquially** 副口語で, 口語的に

- [ ] **combination** 名①結合(状態, 行為), 団結 ②連合, 同盟

- [ ] **combined** 形①結び付いた, 混ぜ合わさった ②複合の, 連合の, 共同の ③一体化した, 統合された

□ **come apart** バラバラになる

□ **come into effect [force]** 〔法律・規則などが〕効力を発する, 施行される, 成立する

□ **come on the scene** 登場する, 姿を現す

□ **come up** 〔問題などが〕持ち上がる, 〔議題などが〕取り上げられる, 話題に出る

□ **comic books** マンガ本

□ **comics** 名 マンガ, マンガ本

□ **coming** 動 come（来る）の現在分詞 形 今度の, 来たるべき 名 到来, 来ること

□ **commodity** 名 商品, 日用品, 産物, 必需品

□ **communication** 名 伝えること, 伝導, 連絡

□ **community with a shared destiny** 運命共同体

□ **company labor union** 企業組合

□ **company men** 会社人間

□ **company spirit** 企業精神

□ **comparison** 名 比較, 対照

□ **compensate** 動 ①補う ②補償する, 補正する

□ **competition** 名 競争, 競合, コンペ

□ **competitive** 形 競争の, 競争心の強い, (品質などが) 他に負けない

□ **competitiveness** 名 競争力

□ **complain** 動 ①不平 [苦情] を言う, ぶつぶつ言う ②(病状などを) 訴える

□ **complete** 形 完全な, まったくの, 完成した 動 完成させる

□ **component** 名 構成要素, 部品, 成分

□ **composition** 名 構成, 組織, 配合

□ **concentrated** 動 concentrate（一点に集める）の過去, 過去分詞 形 ①集中した ②凝縮された, 高濃度の, 濃厚な

□ **concentration** 名 ①集中, 集中力, 集合 ②濃縮, 濃度

□ **concept** 名 ①概念, 観念, テーマ ②(計画案などの) 基本的な方向

□ **concern** 動 ①関係する, 《be -ed in [with] ～》～に関係している ②心配させる, 《be -ed about [for] ～》～を心配する 名 ①関心事 ②関心, 心配 ③関係, 重要性

□ **conclude** 動 ①終える, 完結する ②結論を下す

□ **condition** 名 ①(健康) 状態, 境遇 ②《-s》状況, 様子 ③条件 動 適応させる, 条件づける

□ **conditioner** 名 調節器具, 冷房装置

□ **conduct** 名 ①行い, 振る舞い ②指導, 指揮 動 ①指導する ②実施する, 処理 [処置] する

□ **conference** 名 ①会議, 協議, 相談 ②協議会

□ **confidence** 名 自信, 確信, 信頼, 信用度

□ **connected** 動 connect（つながる）の過去, 過去分詞 形 結合した, 関係のある

□ **conquer** 動 征服する, 制圧する

□ **consciousness** 名 意識, 自覚, 気づいていること

□ **consecutive** 形 連続した, 立て続けの

□ **construction** 名 構造, 建設, 工事, 建物

□ **construction bond** 建設公債

□ **consumer** 名 消費者

□ **consumer durable** 耐久消費財

□ **consumer electronics** 家電 [家庭電化・家庭用電気] 製品

□ **consumer product** 消費財, 消費者 (向け) 製品

□ **consumer-product purpose**

消費者製品用とする，民生用

- [ ] **consumption** 图 ①消費，消費量 ②食べること
- [ ] **contain** 動 ①含む，入っている ②（感情などを）抑える
- [ ] **context** 图 文脈，前後関係，コンテクスト
- [ ] **continuous** 形 連続的な，継続する，絶え間ない
- [ ] **continuously** 副 連続して，絶え間なく，変わりなく
- [ ] **contract** 图 契約（書），協定 動 ①契約する ②縮小する
- [ ] **contrast** 图 対照，対比 動 対照させる，よい対象となる
- [ ] **contribute** 動 ①貢献する ②寄稿する ③寄付する
- [ ] **control** 動 ①管理［支配］する ②抑制する，コントロールする 图 ①管理，支配（力）②抑制 **get out of control** 手に負えなくなる，コントロール［抑え］が利かなくなる
- [ ] **convertibility** 图 ①転換［交換］可能性 ②（通貨の）兌換性
- [ ] **convoy system** 護送船団方式
- [ ] **cooperation** 图 ①協力，協業，協調 ②協同組合
- [ ] **coordinate** 图 ①座標 ②調和よく組み合わされたもの，コーディネート 形 ①（等級・重要度などが）等位の ②座標の 動 ①調和的になる，同格になる ②調整する，協調させる
- [ ] **coordinated intervention** 協調介入
- [ ] **cope** 動 うまく処理する，対処する
- [ ] **core** 图 核心，中心，芯
- [ ] **corona** 图 コロナウイルス（= coronavirus）
- [ ] **coronavirus** 图 《医》コロナウイルス
- [ ] **corporate** 形 団体［共同］の，会社の
- [ ] **corporate financing** 企業金融

- [ ] **corporate profit** 企業収益
- [ ] **corporate restructuring** 企業再建，企業再構築
- [ ] **corporate results** 企業の業績
- [ ] **corporate sector** 法人［企業］部門
- [ ] **corporate takeover** 企業の乗っ取り
- [ ] **corporation** 图 法人，（株式）会社，公団，社団法人
- [ ] **correct** 形 正しい，適切な，りっぱな 動（誤りを）訂正する，直す
- [ ] **cosmetic** 图 化粧品 形 美容の，表面的な
- [ ] **cost** 图 ①値段，費用 ②損失，犠牲 動（金・費用が）かかる，（～を）要する，（人に金額を）費やさせる
- [ ] **cover** 動 ①覆う，包む，隠す ②扱う，（～に）わたる，及ぶ ③代わりを務める ④補う 图 ①覆い，カバー
- [ ] **Covid-19** 略 新型コロナウイルス感染症《2019年12月に中国の湖北省武漢市で発生したとされ，2021年1月現在，多くの国で流行している》（= coronavirus disease 2019）
- [ ] **crash** 動 ①（人・乗り物が）衝突する，墜落する ②大きな音を立ててぶつかる［壊れる］图 ①激突，墜落 ②（壊れるときの）すさまじい音
- [ ] **create** 動 創造する，生み出す，引き起こす
- [ ] **creation** 图 創造［物］
- [ ] **creative destruction** 創造的破壊
- [ ] **credit risk** 信用リスク
- [ ] **creditworthiness** 图 信用力，信用度
- [ ] **crisis** 图 ①危機，難局 ②重大局面
- [ ] **criteria** 图 基準（criterionの複数形）**age criteria** 年齢基準［制限］
- [ ] **critical** 形 ①批評の，批判的な ②危機的な，重大な
- [ ] **criticism** 图 批評，非難，反論，評論

□ **criticize** 動 ①非難する，あら探しをする ②酷評する ③批評する

□ **cross-held share** 持ち合い株

□ **cross-holding share** 株式の持ち合い

□ **cross-shareholdings** 名 (企業間の) 株式持ち合い

□ **crown** 名 ①冠 ②《the –》王位 ③頂，頂上 動 戴冠する［させる］

□ **cultural** 形 文化の，文化的な

□ **currency** 名 ①通貨，貨幣 ②流通，通用すること

□ **current** 形 現在の，目下の，通用［流通］している 名 流れ，電流，風潮

□ **cut back on** ～を削減する

□ **cutting** 動 cut (切る) の現在分詞 名 ①切ること，裁断，カッティング ②(新聞などの) 切り抜き，(挿し木用の) 切り枝

D

□ **Daiei** 名 ダイエー《スーパーマーケットの「ダイエー」などを運営する日本の企業》

□ **daily** 形 毎日の，日常の 副 毎日，日ごとに 名《-lies》日刊新聞

□ **damage** 名 損害，損傷 動 損害を与える，損なう

□ **deal** 動 ①分配する ②《– with [in]》～を扱う 名 ①取引，扱い ②(不特定の) 量，額 **a good [great] deal (of ～)** かなり［ずいぶん・大量］(の～)，多額(の～)

□ **dealing** 熟 **put off dealing with** (問題) の対処を先送りにする

□ **debt** 名 ①借金，負債 ②恩義，借り

□ **debut** 名 デビュー，初登場 動 デビューする

□ **decade** 名 10年間

□ **decades later** 数十年後に

□ **deceleration** 名 減速

□ **decide to do** ～することに決める

□ **decided** 動 decide (決定する) の過去，過去分詞 形 はっきりした，断固とした

□ **declare** 動 ①宣言する ②断言する ③(税関で) 申告する

□ **declare a state of emergency** 緊急事態宣言を発令する

□ **decline** 動 ①断る ②傾く ③衰える 名 ①傾くこと ②下り坂，衰え，衰退

□ **decrease** 動 減少する 名 減少

□ **deepen** 動 深くする，深める

□ **default** 名 ①デフォルト，初期値，初期設定 ②(義務などの) 怠慢，不履行 ③不参加 動 ①(義務・債務などを) 怠る ②デフォルトに設定する

□ **defeat** 動 ①打ち破る，負かす ②だめにする 名 ①敗北 ②挫折

□ **deficit** 名 赤字，不足 (額)

□ **define** 動 ①定義する，限定する ②～の顕著な特性である

□ **deflation** 名 ①デフレ，物価の下落，通貨収縮 ②ガスなどを抜くこと，収縮

□ **deflationary spiral** デフレスパイラル，景気減速

□ **degree** 名 ①程度，階級，位，身分 ②(温度・角度の) 度

□ **deliver** 動 ①配達する，伝える ②達成する，果たす

□ **demand** 動 ①要求する，尋ねる ②必要とする 名 ①要求，請求 ②需要

□ **democratic** 形 ①民主主義の，民主制の ②民主的な

□ **democratization** 名 民主化

□ **democratize** 動 民主化する

□ **department manager** 部長

□ **depend** 動《– on [upon] ～》①～を頼る，～をあてにする ②～による

100

- □ **dependence** 名 依存, 頼ること

- □ **deplete** 動 からにする, 使い果たす

- □ **depopulation** 名 ①人口(の)減少 ②〔人口の減少による〕過疎(化)

- □ **deposit** 動 ①置く ②預金する ③手付金を払う 名 ①預金, 預かり金 ②手付金

- □ **depositor** 名 預金者, 供託者

- □ **deregulate** 動 規制を撤廃［解除］する, 自由化する

- □ **deregulation** 名 規制緩和, 自由化

- □ **describe** 動 (言葉で)描写する, 特色を述べる, 説明する

- □ **design** 動 設計する, 企てる 名 デザイン, 設計(図)

- □ **designate** 動 ①示す ②(～と)称する ③指名する

- □ **desperate** 形 ①絶望的な, 見込みのない ②ほしくてたまらない, 必死の

- □ **despite** 前 ～にもかかわらず

- □ **destabilize** 動 ～の安定性を損なう, ～を不安定にする［陥れる］

- □ **destination** 名 行き先, 目的地

- □ **destiny** 名 運命, 宿命

- □ **destroy** 動 破壊する, 絶滅させる, 無効にする

- □ **destruction** 名 破壊(行為・状態)

- □ **destruction of the ozone layer** オゾン層破壊

- □ **deteriorating** 形 悪化している, 衰えている

- □ **develop** 動 ①発達する［させる］ ②開発する

- □ **developed economy** 先進国の経済, 先進経済

- □ **developed nation** 先進国

- □ **developing** 動 develop (発達する)の現在分詞 形 発展［開発］途上の

- □ **development** 名 ①発達, 発展 ②開発

- □ **devote** 動 ①(～を…に)捧げる ②《 – oneself to ～》～に専念する

- □ **difficulty** 名 ①むずかしさ ②難局, 支障, 苦情, 異議 ③《-ties》財政困難

- □ **digital** 形 ①数字の, 数字表示の, デジタルの ②指の, 指状の

- □ **digital consumer electronics** デジタル家電

- □ **direct** 形 まっすぐな, 直接の, 率直な, 露骨な 副 まっすぐに, 直接に 動 ①指導する, 監督する ②(目・注意・努力などを)向ける

- □ **direct financing** 直接金融

- □ **directed at** 《be –》～をターゲットにする

- □ **directly** 副 ①じかに ②まっすぐに ③ちょうど

- □ **director** 名 管理者, 指導者, 監督

- □ **disaster** 名 災害, 災難, まったくの失敗

- □ **discount** 名 ディスカウント, 割引 動 割引する, 軽視する

- □ **discussion** 名 討議, 討論

- □ **disease** 名 ①病気 ②(社会や精神の)不健全な状態

- □ **disorder** 名 混乱, 無秩序, 乱雑 動 乱す

- □ **disparity** 名 格差, 不均衡

- □ **disperse** 動 追い散らす, 分散させる

- □ **disposable** 形 ①自由に使える, 処分できる ②使い捨ての

- □ **disposable income** 可処分所得

- □ **disposal** 名 処分, 廃棄

- □ **dispose** 動 ①処理する, 捨てる ②配置する

- □ **dispute** 名 論争, 議論 動 反論する, 論争する

- □ **distribution** 名 ①分配 ②配布, 配給 ③流通 ④分布, 区分

A B C D E F G H I J K L M N O P Q R S T U V W X Y Z

- **dividend** 名《金融》配当（金）
- **division of labor** 分業体制
- **doing** 既 start doing ～し始める stop doing ～するのをやめる
- **dollar-denominated assets** ドル建て資産
- **domestic** 形①家庭の ②国内の, 自国の, 国産の
- **domestic consumption** 国内消費
- **domestic demand** 内需
- **Doraemon** 名ドラえもん《藤子・F・不二雄による日本の児童SFマンガ。および, 作品内に登場する主人公（未来からやって来たネコ型ロボット）の名前》
- **double** 形①2倍の, 二重の ②対の 副①2倍に ②対で 動①2倍になる［する］ ②兼ねる
- **doubling** 名2倍にすること, 倍加
- **down** 動 push down 押し倒す
- **downsizing** 名〔企業・組織などの〕人員削減, 経営合理化
- **downward** 形下方の, 下向きの, 下降する, 以後の 副下方へ, 下向きに, 堕落して, ～以後
- **drag** 動①引きずる ②のろのろ動く［動かす］名①引きずること ②のろのろすること
- **Dragon Ball** ドラゴンボール《鳥山明による日本のマンガ・アニメ作品。および, その作中に登場するアイテムの名称》
- **drinking** 動drink（飲む）の現在分詞 名飲むこと, 飲酒
- **driven** 動drive（車で行く）の過去分詞
- **drop in value** 《a–》価値の低下［目減り］, 価格の下落
- **dropout** 名①〔競争などからの〕脱落（者）②〔学校を卒業する前の〕中途退学（者）③〔既成社会からの〕脱退（者）

- **drove** 動drive（車で行く）の過去
- **due** 形予定された, 期日のきている, 支払われるべき 名当然の権利 due to ～によって, ～が原因で
- **durable** 形永続する, 耐久性のある
- **dynamic** 形活動的な, 動的な, ダイナミックな
- **dynamic engagement of all citizens** 一億総活躍
- **dysfunction** 名①機能障害［不全］②〔社会構成単位の〕逆機能

E

- **each other** お互いに
- **eager** 形①熱心な ②《be–for ～》～を切望している,《be–to ～》しきりに～したがっている
- **early retirement** 早期退職
- **earn** 動①儲ける, 稼ぐ ②（名声を）博す
- **earnings** 名所得, 収入, 稼ぎ
- **earthquake** 名地震, 大変動
- **ease** 名安心, 気楽 動安心させる, 楽にする, ゆるめる
- **eastern** 形①東方の, 東向きの ②東洋の, 東洋風の
- **easy-money policy** 金融緩和政策, 低金利政策
- **economic** 形経済学の, 経済上の
- **economic boom** 好景気, 好況
- **economic growth** 経済成長（率）, 高度成長, 経済発展
- **economic indicator** 経済指標
- **Economic Partnership Agreement (EPA)** 経済連携協定
- **economic superpower** 経済大国
- **Economic White Paper** 経済

白書

- □ **economy** 名 ①経済, 財政 ②節約
- □ **education** 名 教育, 教養
- □ **effect** 名 ①影響, 効果, 結果 ②実施, 発効 動 もたらす, 達成する
- □ **effective** 形 効果的である, 有効である
- □ **effectively** 副 効果的に, 効率的に
- □ **effectiveness** 名 有効性
- □ **efficiency** 名 ①能率, 効率 ②能力
- □ **efficient** 形 ①効率的な, 有効な ②有能な, 敏腕な
- □ **efficiently** 副 効果的に, 能率的に
- □ **effort** 名 努力 (の成果)
- □ **elderly** 形 かなり年配の, 初老の 名 《the –》お年寄り
- □ **electric** 形 電気の, 電動の
- □ **electric appliance** 電気器具 [製品]
- □ **electric-power generation** 発電
- □ **electrical** 形 電気の, 電気に関する
- □ **electrical machinery** 電気機械
- □ **electricity** 名 電気
- □ **electronic** 形 電子工学の, エレクトロニクスの
- □ **electronics** 名 エレクトロニクス, 電子工学, 電子機器
- □ **electronics technology** エレクトロニクス技術
- □ **eliminate** 動 削除 [排除・除去] する, 撤廃する
- □ **embark** 動 乗船する, 着手する, 始める
- □ **emerge** 動 現れる, 浮かび上がる, 明らかになる
- □ **emergency** 名 非常時, 緊急時 形 緊急の

- □ **emergency loan** 緊急融資, つなぎ融資
- □ **emission** 名 放出, 放射, 発射, 発光, 排気
- □ **emotionally** 副 感情的に, 情緒的に
- □ **employee** 名 従業員, 会社員, 被雇用者
- □ **employer** 名 雇主, 使用 [利用] する人
- □ **employment** 名 ①雇用 ②仕事, 職
- □ **employment agency staff** 派遣社員
- □ **empower** 動 ～する権限 [能力・機能] を与える
- □ **enable** 動 (～することを) 可能にする, 容易にする
- □ **enact** 動 制定する, 成立させる be enacted 起こる
- □ **encourage** 動 ①勇気づける ②促進する, 助長する
- □ **encouraging** 動 encourage (勇気づける) の過去, 過去分詞 形 元気づける
- □ **end** 熟 at the end of ～の終わりに end up 結局～になる in the end とうとう, 結局, ついに
- □ **endure** 動 ①我慢する, 耐え忍ぶ ②持ちこたえる
- □ **energy-efficient** 形 燃費がよい, エネルギー効率がよい
- □ **engagement** 名 婚約, 約束
- □ **engine** 名 エンジン, 機関, (精巧な) 機械装置
- □ **enormous** 形 ばく大な, 非常に大きい, 巨大な
- □ **enter into** ～に入る
- □ **entertainment** 名 ①楽しみ, 娯楽 ②もてなし, 歓待
- □ **environment** 名 ①環境 ②周囲 (の状況), 情勢

103

☐ **environment-friendly** 形 環境
にやさしい

☐ **environmental** 形 ①環境の, 周
囲の ②環境保護の

☐ **equal** 形 等しい, 均等な, 平等な
動 匹敵する, 等しい 名 同等のもの
[人]

☐ **equipment** 名 装置, 機材, 道具,
設備

☐ **equity** 名 ①公正 ②株主資本 ③
株(式)

☐ **equity ratio** 自己資本比率

☐ **equivalent** 形 ①同等の, 等しい
②同意義の 名 同等のもの, 等価なも
の

☐ **essential** 形 本質的な, 必須の 名
本質, 要点, 必需品

☐ **establish** 動 確立する, 立証する,
設置[設立]する

☐ **estate** 名 不動産, 財産, 遺産, 地所,
土地 real estate 不動産, 土地

☐ **EU** 略 欧州連合 (= European
Union)

☐ **even if** たとえ~でも

☐ **eventually** 副 結局は

☐ **ever more** これまで以上に

☐ **ever since** それ以来ずっと

☐ **everyday** 形 毎日の, 日々の

☐ **everywhere** 副 どこにいても, い
たるところに

☐ **evolution** 名 ①進化 ②展開, 旋
回 ③(熱などの) 発生

☐ **exacerbate** 動 [悪い状況をさら
に] 悪化させる, 深刻にする

☐ **exact** 形 正確な, 厳密な, きちょう
めんな

☐ **examine** 動 試験する, 調査[検査]
する, 診察する

☐ **example** 熟 for example たとえ
ば

☐ **exceed** 動 (程度・限度などを) 超
える, 上回る, 勝る

☐ **except** 前 ~を除いて, ~のほか
は 接 ~ということを除いて except
for ~を除いて, ~がなければ

☐ **exception** 名 例外, 除外, 異論

☐ **excess** 名 ①超過, 過剰 ②不節制
形 超過の, 過剰な, 余分の in excess
of ~より多くを, ~を超えて

☐ **excess capital investment**
過剰設備投資

☐ **excess employment** 過剰雇
用

☐ **excessive** 形 度を超えた, 行き過
ぎた, 極端な

☐ **excessive debt** 過剰債務

☐ **excessive inflow** 転入超過《転
入者が転出者を上回ること》

☐ **exchange rate** 為替レート

☐ **exchange-rate risk** 為替リスク

☐ **execlude** 動 (~を)排除する, 除
外する, 考慮しない

☐ **executive** 形 実行の, 執行の
名 ①高官, 実行委員 ②重役, 役員,
幹部

☐ **exempt** 動 免除する 形 免除され
た

☐ **existing** 動 exist (存在する)の現
在分詞 形 現存の, 現在の, 現行の

☐ **expand** 動 ①広げる, 拡張[拡大]
する ②発展させる, 拡充する

☐ **expansion** 名 拡大, 拡張, 展開

☐ **expansionary** 形 拡大性の, 拡大
経済の, インフレの

☐ **expect** 動 予期[予測]する, (当然
のこととして)期待する

☐ **expenditure** 名 ①支出(額), 支
払い, 経費, 費用 ②(国家の) 歳出, 支
出

☐ **explosive** 形 ①爆発性の, 爆発的
な ②一触即発の 名 爆発物, 爆薬

☐ **export** 動 輸出する 名 輸出, 国外
への持ち出し

☐ **export industry** 輸出産業

□ **export-led economy** 輸出主導型経済

□ **exporter** 图輸出業者

□ **exposed** 動expose（さらす）の過去, 過去分詞 形①雨風［光, 攻撃, 危険］にさらされた ②露出した, 無防備な ③露呈した, 発覚した

□ **express** 動表現する, 述べる 形①明白な ②急行の 图速達便, 急行列車 副速達で, 急行で

□ **expressway** 图高速道路

□ **extend** 動①伸ばす, 延長［延期］する ②（範囲が）およぶ, 広がる, （期間などが）わたる

□ **external** 图外部, 外観, 外面 形外部の, 外側の, 外国との

□ **extra-curricular study** 課外学習, 学校外での学習

□ **extremely** 副非常に, 極度に

□ **eye** 熟keep an eye on ～から目を離さない

F

□ **facility** 图①《-ties》施設, 設備 ②器用さ, 容易さ

□ **fact** 熟in fact つまり, 実は, 要するに

□ **factor** 图要因, 要素, 因子

□ **factory** 图工場, 製造所

□ **fail** 動①失敗する, 落第する［させる］②《- to ～》～し損なう, ～できない ③失望させる 图失敗, 落第点

□ **failure** 图①失敗, 落第 ②不足, 欠乏 ③停止, 減退

□ **fairness** 图公平さ, 公明正大さ

□ **fall behind** 取り残される, 後れを取る

□ **fall into** ～に陥る, ～してしまう

□ **fall off** 落ちる, 減る, 衰退する

□ **fallen** 動fall（落ちる）の過去分詞 形落ちた, 倒れた

□ **falling-off** 图減少, 減退

□ **fallout** 图副産物, 副次的な［予期しない］影響

□ **familiarity** 图熟知, 親しさ, なれなれしさ familiarity with ～に熟知していること

□ **family-like harmony** 家族的な「和」

□ **fashion** 图①流行, 方法, はやり ②流行のもの（特に服装）in fashion 流行して, はやって

□ **fast-growing country** 急成長している（成長著しい）国

□ **fear** 图①恐れ ②心配, 不安 動①恐れる ②心配する

□ **feature** 图①特徴, 特色 ②顔の一部,《-s》顔立ち ③（ラジオ・テレビ・新聞などの）特集 動①（～の）特徴になる ②呼び物にする

□ **feature-length** 形〔映画などが〕長編の

□ **feeling** 動feel（感じる）の現在分詞 图①感じ, 気持ち ②触感, 知覚 ③同情, 思いやり, 感受性 形感じる, 感じやすい, 情け深い

□ **female** 形女性の, 婦人の, 雌の 图婦人, 雌

□ **fertilizer** 图①（化学）肥料 ②豊かにする人［物］③受精媒介者

□ **fever** 图①熱, 熱狂 ②熱病 speculative fever 投機熱 動発熱させる, 熱狂させる

□ **fierce** 形どう猛な, 荒々しい, すさまじい, 猛烈な

□ **fight back** 反撃に転じる, 応戦する

□ **figure** 图①人［物］の姿, 形 ②図（形）③数字 動①描写する, 想像する ②計算する ③目立つ, （～として）現れる figure out 理解する, ～であるとわかる, （原因などを）解明する

□ **file** 图ファイル, 書類綴じ, 縦列 動①とじ込む, 保管する ②削り取る,

105

やすりをかける

- [ ] **film** 名①フィルム，映画 ②膜 動映画を製作［撮影］する

- [ ] **final** 形最後の，決定的な 名①最後のもの ②期末［最終］試験 ③《-s》決勝戦

- [ ] **finance** 名①財政，財務 ②（銀行からの）資金，融資 ③《-s》財政状態，財源 動資金を融通する

- [ ] **finance minister** 財務大臣，大蔵大臣

- [ ] **financial** 形①財務（上）の，金融（上）の ②金融関係者の

- [ ] **financial crisis** 経営［金融・財政（的）］危機，金融不安［恐慌］

- [ ] **financial institution** 金融機関

- [ ] **financial product** 金融商品

- [ ] **Financial Services Agency** 金融庁

- [ ] **financing** 名融資，資金調達，資金繰り

- [ ] **finished goods [products]** 完成品

- [ ] **first** 熟 **at first** 最初は，初めのうちは **for the first time** 初めて

- [ ] **First Oil Crisis** 第一次石油危機

- [ ] **fiscal** 形財務の，財政上の，会計の，国庫の

- [ ] **fiscal deficit** 財政赤字

- [ ] **fiscal policy** 財政政策

- [ ] **fiscal reform** 財政改革

- [ ] **fiscal stimulus package** 財政刺激策

- [ ] **fiscal year**〔政府や自治体の〕会計年度，財政年度

- [ ] **fishery** 名漁業，水産業

- [ ] **five advanced nations** 先進5ヵ国，主要5ヵ国（G5）《米国・英国・ドイツ・フランス・日本》

- [ ] **flare-up** 名〔問題・病気などの〕激発，突発，カッと怒ること

- [ ] **flexible** 形①（物が）曲がりやすい，しなやかな ②（考えなどが）柔軟性のある，順応性のある ③（予定・計画などが）融通のきく ④弾力的な，可塑性のある

- [ ] **flexible fiscal policy** 機動的な財政政策

- [ ] **floating** 形浮いている，流動的な

- [ ] **focus** 名①焦点，ピント ②関心の的，着眼点 ③中心 動①焦点を合わせる ②（関心・注意を）集中させる

- [ ] **followed by** その後に～が続いて

- [ ] **following** 動 follow（ついていく）の現在分詞 形《the -》次の，次に続く 名《the -》下記のもの，以下に述べるもの

- [ ] **for example** たとえば

- [ ] **for the first time** 初めて

- [ ] **for ~ years** ～年間，～年にわたって

- [ ] **force** 名力，勢い 動①強制する，力ずくで～する，余儀なく～させる ②押しやる，押し込む

- [ ] **fore** 形前の，前方の 副前に，前方に 名《the -》前面，前部

- [ ] **forecast** 名予想，予測，天気予報，先見 動①予見する ②前もって計画をたてる，予定する ③予測する，予報する

- [ ] **foreign exchange market** 外国為替市場

- [ ] **foreign-exchange loss** 外国為替差損

- [ ] **foreign-exchange risk** 外国為替リスク

- [ ] **foremost** 形真っ先の，第一の 副真っ先に，第一に

- [ ] **foreword** 名〔本などの〕前書き，序文

- [ ] **form** 名①形，形式 ②書式 動形づくる

- [ ] **forum** 名公開討論（の場），公共広場

- [ ] **forward** 形①前方の，前方へ向か

う ②将来の ③先の 副①前方に ②
将来に向けて ③先へ，進んで 動①
転送する ②進める 名前衛

- [ ] **foster** 動①育てる，促進させる ②
心に抱く 形里親の

- [ ] **framework** 名骨組み，構造，組織

- [ ] **freedom** 名①自由 ②束縛がない
こと

- [ ] **freeter** 名フリーター《和製英語》

- [ ] **freezing** 形酷寒の，こごえるよう
な

- [ ] **frequently** 副頻繁に，しばしば

- [ ] **friction** 名摩擦，不和

- [ ] **from abroad** 海外から

- [ ] **from this point on** この地点か
ら先は

- [ ] **from ～ to …** ～から…まで

- [ ] **fuel-cell hybrid vehicle** 燃料
電池自動車

- [ ] **fuel-efficient** 形燃費がよい，低
燃費の

- [ ] **Fukushima Daiichi nuclear
power plant of Tokyo
Electric Power Company
(TEPCO)** 東京電力福島第一原子力
発電所

- [ ] **fulfill** 動（義務・約束を）果たす，（要
求・条件を）満たす

- [ ] **full-scale** 形全面的な，本格的な，
実物大の

- [ ] **full-time** 名常勤の，専任の

- [ ] **function** 動働く，機能する 名機
能，作用

- [ ] **fund** 名①資金，基金，財源 ②金
③公債，国債 動①資金を出す ②長
期公債の借り換えをする

- [ ] **further** 形いっそう遠い，その上の，
なおいっそうの 副いっそう遠く，そ
の上に，もっと 動促進する

- [ ] **future** 熟 in the future 将来は
well into the future 将来にわたっ
ても

G

- [ ] **G5** 略《the – 》主要5カ国《米国・英国・
ドイツ・フランス・日本》(= Group
of Five)

- [ ] **gap** 名ギャップ，隔たり，すき間
動すき間ができる

- [ ] **garner** 動〔情報を〕集める

- [ ] **gas** 名①ガス，気体 ②ガソリン
動ガス［ガソリン］を供給する

- [ ] **GDP** 略国内総生産 (= gross
domestic product)

- [ ] **general** 形①全体の，一般の，普
通の ②おおよその ③（職位の）高い，
上級の **general account** 一般会計

- [ ] **general account** 一般会計

- [ ] **general machinery** 一般機械

- [ ] **general price deflation** 一般
物価デフレ

- [ ] **generation** 名発生，生成

- [ ] **German** 形ドイツ（人・語）の
名①ドイツ人 ②ドイツ語

- [ ] **get out of** ～から下車する，～か
ら取り出す，～から外へ出る［抜け出
る］

- [ ] **get out of control** 手に負えな
くなる，コントロール［抑え］が利か
なくなる

- [ ] **get rid of** ～を取り除く

- [ ] **get someone to volunteer
for** （人に）～を志願させる

- [ ] **get worse** 悪化する

- [ ] **gigantic** 形巨大な，膨大な

- [ ] **Gini coefficient** ジニ係数，国民
所得分配係数《社会における所得分配
の不平等さを測る尺度の一つ》

- [ ] **give birth to** ～を生む

- [ ] **give up** あきらめる，やめる

- [ ] **global** 形地球（上）の，地球規模の，
世界的な，国際的な

- [ ] **global warming** 地球温暖化

- [ ] **gloomy** 形①憂うつな，陰気な ②

うす暗い

- [ ] **GNP** 略国民総生産（＝ gross national product）
- [ ] **go ahead** 進んで行う，思い切って〜する
- [ ] **go bankrupt** 倒産する
- [ ] **go into** 〜に入る，〜に陥る
- [ ] **go on** 続く，進み続ける，起こる
- [ ] **go on to** 〜に移る，〜に取り掛かる
- [ ] **go out to work** 仕事に出かける
- [ ] **go through** 通り抜ける，一つずつ順番に検討する
- [ ] **gold** 名金，金貨，金製品，金色 形金の，金製の，金色の
- [ ] **goods** 名①商品，品物 ②財産，所有物
- [ ] **govern** 動治める，管理する，支配する
- [ ] **governance** 名①〔国家・君主などが国・国民などに対して行う政治的な〕支配，統治 ②〔学校・企業などの〕管理，運営
- [ ] **governance function** ガバナンス機能
- [ ] **government** 名政治，政府，支配
- [ ] **government bond** 国債
- [ ] **government debt** 政府債
- [ ] **government deficit** 政府赤字，政府赤字
- [ ] **governor** 名①知事 ②支配者，（学校・病院・官庁などの）長
- [ ] **gradually** 副だんだんと
- [ ] **graduate** 動卒業する 名卒業生，（〜学校の）出身者
- [ ] **graduation** 名卒業（式）
- [ ] **grail** 名〔努力を要する〕究極の目的
- [ ] **grant** 動①許可する，承諾する ②授与する，譲渡する ③（なるほどと）認める 名授与されたもの
- [ ] **granted** 熟 take 〜 for granted 〜を当然のことと思う

- [ ] **great** 熟 a great deal 多くのこと［もの］ a great deal of 多量の，大量の
- [ ] **Great East Japan Earthquake** 《the –》東日本大震災
- [ ] **greenhouse** 名温室 形温室効果の
- [ ] **greenhouse gases** 温室効果ガス
- [ ] **gross** 形①総計の，全体の ②ひどい，（食べ物が）粗末な，不快な 名総計，総予算，全体
- [ ] **gross national product** 国民総生産（GNP）
- [ ] **grouping** 名グループ，グループ分け
- [ ] **growing** 動 grow（成長する）の現在分詞 形成長期にある，大きくなりつつある
- [ ] **growth** 名成長，発展 形成長している
- [ ] **growth industry** 成長産業
- [ ] **growth rate** 成長［増加］率［速度］
- [ ] **growth strategy designed to stimulate private-sector investment** 民間投資を喚起する成長戦略
- [ ] **guidance** 名案内，手引き，指導

H

- [ ] **haken-giri** 名派遣切り
- [ ] **halt** 動①止まる，停止する ②もたもたする，筋が通らない 名中止，休止
- [ ] **halve** 動①半分になる ②半分にする，等分する，半減させる
- [ ] **hand** 熟 on the other hand 一方，他方では
- [ ] **handle** 名取っ手，握り 動①手を

触れる ②操縦する, 取り扱う

- [ ] **hard to** 〜し難い
- [ ] **hardworking** 形 勤勉な, よく働く
- [ ] **harm** 名 害, 損害, 危害 動 傷つける, 損なう
- [ ] **harmonious** 形 調和のとれた, 仲むつまじい
- [ ] **harmony** 名 調和, 一致, ハーモニー
- [ ] **Haruhiko Kuroda** 黒田東彦 (1944–)《第31代日本銀行総裁》
- [ ] **have no choice but to** 〜するしかない
- [ ] **have nothing to do with** 〜と何の関係もない
- [ ] **have worry about** 〜に不安を抱く[持つ]
- [ ] **Hayao Miyazaki** 宮崎駿 (1941–)《日本のアニメーション作家, 映画監督》
- [ ] **Hayato Ikeda** 池田勇人 (1899–1965)《第58〜60代内閣総理大臣》
- [ ] **headquarter** 動 〜の本部を置く
- [ ] **headquarters** 名 本部, 司令部, 本署
- [ ] **health care** 医療
- [ ] **heavy-chemicals** 形 重化学の
- [ ] **helping** 動 help (助ける) の現在分詞 名 ①助力, 手助け ②(食べ物の) ひと盛り, 1杯, お代わり 形 救いの, 助けの
- [ ] **high-quality** 形 高品質の
- [ ] **high-tech** 形 〔技術が〕ハイテクの, 先端技術の
- [ ] **high-value-added** 形 高付加価値の, 付加価値の高い
- [ ] **highly** 副 ①大いに, 非常に ②高度に, 高位に ③高く評価して, 高価で
- [ ] **Highway Public Corporation** 道路関係公団

- [ ] **hikikomori** 名 ひきこもり
- [ ] **hinder** 動 妨害する, じゃまする
- [ ] **hire** 動 雇う, 賃借りする 名 雇用, 賃借り, 使用料
- [ ] **Hiroshima** 名 広島《地名》
- [ ] **Hitachi** 名 日立製作所《茨城県日立市で創業した世界有数の総合電機メーカー》
- [ ] **hollow** 名 ①へこみ ②空白 形 うつろな, くぼんだ
- [ ] **hollowing out of industry** 産業の空洞化
- [ ] **holy** 形 聖なる, 神聖な
- [ ] **Holy Grail** 困難な探求の対象, 渇望の品, 至高の目標《元の意味である「聖杯」を探求する伝説から転じて》
- [ ] **home** 熟 at home 自宅で, 在宅して, 自国で stay at home 家にこもる, 国内にとどまる
- [ ] **home (electric [electronic]) appliance** 家庭電気製品, 家電器具[製品]
- [ ] **home electronics** 家電[家庭電化・家庭用電気]製品
- [ ] **home video game** 家庭用ビデオゲーム
- [ ] **homemaker** 名 専業主婦
- [ ] **Honda Motor** 名 本田技研工業, ホンダ《日本の大手輸送機器メーカー》
- [ ] **household** 名 家族, 世帯 形 家族の
- [ ] **housework** 名 家事
- [ ] **hover** 動 ①(ヘリコプター・鳥などが) 停止飛行する, 旋回する, ホバーリングする ②うろつく
- [ ] **how to** 〜する方法
- [ ] **however** 副 たとえ〜でも 接 けれども, だが
- [ ] **Hubei Province** 湖北省《中国の地名》
- [ ] **huge** 形 巨大な, ばく大な

A
B
C
D
E
F
G
H
I
J
K
L
M
N
O
P
Q
R
S
T
U
V
W
X
Y
Z

□ **human resources** 人材, 人的資源

□ **human-resources** 形 人事の, 人材の

□ **hybrid vehicle** ハイブリッド車 [カー]《エンジンと電気モーターの二つの動力を併用して駆動する自動車》

I

□ **ideally** 副 理想的に, 申し分なく

□ **if** 熟 **as if** あたかも〜のように, まるで〜みたいに **even if** たとえ〜でも

□ **imaginative** 形 想像力豊かな

□ **immediate** 形 さっそくの, 即座の, 直接の

□ **impact** 名 影響力, 反響, 効果 動 ①詰め込む ②衝突する

□ **impediment** 名 妨げ, 障害

□ **implement** 名 ①道具 ②履行 動 ①実行する ②道具[手段]を提供する

□ **import** 動 輸入する 名 輸入, 輸入品

□ **importance** 名 重要性, 大切さ

□ **impose** 動 課す, 負わせる, 押しつける

□ **improve** 動 改善する[させる], 進歩する

□ **improvement** 名 改良, 改善

□ **in addition** 加えて, さらに

□ **in addition to** 〜に加えて, さらに

□ **in excess of** 〜より多くを, 〜を超えて

□ **in fact** つまり, 実は, 要するに

□ **in fashion** 流行して, はやって

□ **in order to** 〜するために, 〜しようと

□ **in other words** すなわち, 言い換えれば

□ **in small steps** 少しずつ, だんだんと

□ **in terms of** 〜の言葉で言えば, 〜の点から

□ **in the end** とうとう, 結局, ついに

□ **in the future** 将来は

□ **in the world** 世界で

□ **in this way** このようにして

□ **in turn** 順番に, 立ち代わって

□ **inbound** 形 入ってくる, 到着する

□ **inbound tourists** 訪日外国人旅行客(インバウンド)

□ **Inc.** 略 法人組織の, 有限責任の (= incorporated)

□ **include** 動 含む, 勘定に入れる

□ **including** 動 include (含む) の現在分詞 前 〜を含めて, 込みで

□ **income** 名 収入, 所得, 収益

□ **Income Doubling Plan** 所得倍増計画《1960年に池田内閣の下で策定された長期経済計画》

□ **increase** 動 増加[増強]する, 増やす, 増える 名 増加(量), 増大 **on the increase** 増加して

□ **increasing domestic demand** 内需拡大

□ **increasingly** 副 ますます, だんだん

□ **independence** 名 独立心, 自立

□ **indicator** 名 指標, 指針

□ **indices** 名 index (索引, 指標) の複数形

□ **indirect** 形 間接的な, 二次的な

□ **indirect financing** 間接金融

□ **individual** 形 独立した, 個性的な, 個々の 名 個体, 個人

□ **individuality** 名 個性, 特性, 個人

□ **indoors** 副 室内で, 屋内で

□ **industrial** 形 工業の, 産業の

□ **industrial policy** 産業政策

☐ **industrial production** 鉱工業生産

☐ **Industrial Revitalization Corporation of Japan** 産業再生機構

☐ **industry** 名 産業, 工業

☐ **inefficiency** 名 非能率, 能力不足

☐ **inefficient** 形 効果のない, 能率［効率］の悪い, 不振の

☐ **inequality** 名 ①不平等, 不均衡 ②〈-ties〉起伏, (表面の) 荒いこと ③ (天候・温度の) 変動 ④不等式

☐ **infect** 動 ①感染する, 伝染する ② (病気を) 移す ③影響を及ぼす

☐ **infection** 名 (病気など) 感染, 伝染

☐ **inflation** 名 ①膨張 ②インフレーション《物価の暴騰》

☐ **inflation target** インフレターゲット, インフレ目標

☐ **inflict** 動 ①〔相手にとって嫌なこと・苦痛になることを〕与える, 課する ② (人) を苦しめる, (人) に重荷を負わせる

☐ **inflow** 名 流入 (すること)

☐ **influence** 名 影響, 勢力 動 影響をおよぼす

☐ **infrastructure** 名 社会基盤, インフラ

☐ **initiate** 動 〔通例重要なことを〕始める, 開始する

☐ **initiative** 名 主導権, イニシアチブ

☐ **inject** 動 注射［注入］する

☐ **innovation** 名 ①革新, 刷新 ②新しいもの, 新考案

☐ **inroad** 名《通例 -s》侵入, 進出

☐ **instability** 名 不安定 (性)

☐ **instead** 副 その代わりに

☐ **institution** 名 ①設立, 制定 ②制度, 慣習 ③協会, 公共団体

☐ **instruct** 動 ①教える, 教育する ②指図［命令］する

☐ **insurance** 名 保険

☐ **insure** 動 ①保険をかける ②保証する, 請け合う

☐ **integrate** 動 ①統合する, 一体化する ②溶け込ませる, 溶け込む, 差別をなくす

☐ **intelligent** 形 頭のよい, 聡明な

☐ **"intelligent" consumer electronics** 情報家電

☐ **intense** 形 ①強烈な, 激しい ②感情的な

☐ **intensity** 名 強烈さ, 激しさ

☐ **interdependence** 名〔人・物の〕持ちつ持たれつの関係, 相互依存

☐ **interest payment** 利払い

☐ **interest rate** 金利, 利率

☐ **intermittent** 形 断続的な

☐ **international comparison** 国際比較

☐ **international competitiveness** 国際競争力

☐ **internationalization** 名 国際化

☐ **internationally** 副 国際的に

☐ **interpretation** 名 ①解釈 ②通訳

☐ **intervention** 名 介入, 仲裁, 調停, 干渉

☐ **introduction** 名 紹介, 導入

☐ **invest** 動 投資する, (金・精力など) を注ぐ

☐ **investment** 名 投資, 出資

☐ **involve** 動 ①含む, 伴う ②巻き込む, かかわらせる

☐ **involved** 動 involve (含む) の過去, 過去分詞 形 ①巻き込まれている, 関連する ②入り組んだ, 込み入っている

☐ **iron** 名 ①鉄, 鉄製のもの ②アイロン 形 鉄の, 鉄製の 動 アイロンをかける

☐ **irregular** 形 不規則な, ふぞろいの

☐ **irregular employment** 非正規雇用

☐ **isolated** 動isolate(隔離する)の過去, 過去分詞 形隔離した, 孤立した

☐ **issuance** 名発行, 支給, 発布, 配給

☐ **issue** 名①問題, 論点 ②発行物 ③出口, 流出 動①(〜から)出る, 生じる ②発行する

☐ **It is 〜 for someone to …** (人)が…するのは〜だ

☐ **Itai-Itai Disease** イタイイタイ病《富山県で発生した日本初の公害病》

☐ **itemize** 動項目別[個条書き]にする

☐ **itself** 代それ自体, それ自身

☐ **Iwato Boom** 岩戸景気《1958年7月〜1961年12月まで42ヵ月間続いた高度経済成長時代の好景気》

☐ **Izanagi Boom** いざなぎ景気《1965年11月〜1970年7月まで57ヵ月間続いた高度経済成長時代の好景気》

☐ **Izanami Boom** いざなみ景気《2002年2月〜2008年2月まで73ヵ月間続いた好景気》

J

☐ **Japan** 名日本《国名》

☐ **Japan External Trade Organization (JETRO)** 日本貿易振興機構

☐ **Japan Inc.** 日本株式会社, ジャパン・インク《日本の国民経済を会社に例えて用いられる用語, 概念》

☐ **Japan National Railways** 日本国有鉄道, 国鉄《1987年に分割民営化され消滅した》

☐ **Japan National Tourism Organization** 日本政府観光局《国土交通省(観光庁)所管の独立行政法人》

☐ **Japan premium** ジャパン・プレミアム, 邦銀向け上乗せ金利

☐ **Japan Tobacco and Salt Public Corporation** 日本専売公社《1985年に民営化され, 日本たばこ産業株式会社(JT)が設立された》

☐ **Japan Tourism Agency (JTA)** 観光庁

☐ **Japan-made** 形日本製の

☐ **Japan-U.S. Framework for New Economic Partnership** 日米包括経済協議

☐ **Japanese** 形日本(人・語)の 名①日本人 ②日本語

☐ **Japanese Big Bang** 日本型ビッグバン

☐ **Japanese-made** 形日本製の

☐ **Japanese-style management system** 日本型経営システム

☐ **jewel** 名宝石, 貴重な人[物] 動宝石で飾る

☐ **Jimmu Boom** 神武景気《1965年11月〜1970年7月まで57ヵ月間続いた高度経済成長時代の好景気》

☐ **job counseling** 就職相談

☐ **job placement service** 職業紹介サービス

☐ **jobseeker** 名求職者

☐ **jointly** 副共同で, 一緒に

☐ **JTA** 略観光庁(= Japan Tourism Agency)

☐ **Junichiro Koizumi** 小泉純一郎 (1942–)《第87〜89代内閣総理大臣》

☐ **"just-in-time production" system** ジャスト・イン・タイム方式

K

- □ **kaishaningen** 名会社人間
- □ **kaizen** 名改善, カイゼン
- □ **kanban** 名看板, カンバン
- □ **kanban system** カンバン方式
- □ **Kanebo** 名カネボウ《日本の大手化粧品会社》
- □ **keep an eye on** ～から目を離さない
- □ **keiretsu** 名系列
- □ **kingdom** 名王国
- □ **known as** 《be –》～として知られている
- □ **Korean War** 朝鮮戦争 (1950–53)
- □ **Kyoto** 名京都《地名》
- □ **Kyoto Protocol** 京都議定書《1997年に採択された気候変動枠組条約に関する議定書》

L

- □ **labor** 名労働, 骨折り 動①働く, 努力する, 骨折る ②苦しむ, 悩む
- □ **labor issue** 労働問題
- □ **labor market** 労働市場
- □ **Labor Standards Law** 労働基準法
- □ **labor-management** 形労使の [に関する]
- □ **land myth** 土地神話
- □ **land taxation** 土地税制
- □ **land-holding tax** 地価税, 土地保有税
- □ **land-sharking** 名強引な手口の地上げ
- □ **large** 熟 at large 全体として, 広く
- □ **large-scale** 形大規模の
- □ **last of all** 最後に
- □ **latest** 形①最新の, 最近の ②最も

遅い 副最も遅く, 最後に
- □ **latter** 形①後の, 末の, 後者の ②《the –》後者《代名詞的に用いる》
- □ **launch** 動①(ロケットなどを)打ち上げる, 発射する ②進水させる ③(事業などを)始める
- □ **lay** 動①置く, 横たえる, 敷く ②整える ③卵を産む ④lie (横たわる)の過去 **lay off** レイオフする, 一時解雇する
- □ **layer** 名層, 重ね 動層になる [する]
- □ **LDP** 略《the –》《日》自由民主党, 自民党 (= Liberal Democratic Party)
- □ **lead time** リードタイム, 製品の企画[発注]から生産開始[納品]までに要する時間
- □ **lead to** ～に至る, ～に通じる, ～を引き起こす
- □ **leadership** 名指揮, リーダーシップ
- □ **leading** 動lead (導く)の現在分詞 形主要な, 指導的な, 先頭の **leading role** 主導的役割 **take a leading role in** ～で主導的役割を担う[果たす]
- □ **led** 動lead (導く)の過去, 過去分詞
- □ **legally** 副合法的に, 法律的に
- □ **Lehman Brothers** 《– Holdings Inc.》リーマン・ブラザーズ《かつてアメリカ・ニューヨークに本社を置いていた大手証券持株会社。2008年9月に経営破綻した》
- □ **Lehman shock** リーマン・ショック《リーマン・ブラザーズが2008年9月15日に経営破綻したことを発端とする, 一連の世界規模の金融危機を呼ぶ日本における通称》
- □ **lend** 動貸す, 貸し出す **lend out** 貸し出す
- □ **length** 名長さ, 縦, たけ, 距離
- □ **lent** 動lend (貸す)の過去, 過去分詞
- □ **level** 名①水平, 平面 ②水準 形①水平の, 平たい ②同等[同位]の

動①水平にする ②平等にする

□ **liberal** 形①自由主義の, 進歩的な ②気前のよい 名自由主義者

□ **liberalization** 名自由化

□ **liberalize** 動①自由化する ②（規制などを）緩める

□ **lie** 動①うそをつく ②横たわる, 寝る ③（ある状態に）ある, 存在する lie behind ~の後方［背後］にある 名うそ, 詐欺

□ **life** 熟 bring back to life 生き返る, 息を吹き返す

□ **lifestyle** 名生活様式, ライフスタイル

□ **lifetime** 名①一生, 生涯 ②寿命

□ **lifetime employment** 終身雇用

□ **lift** 動①持ち上げる, 上がる ②取り除く, 撤廃する 名①持ち上げること ②エレベーター, リフト

□ **like this** このような, こんなふうに

□ **likely** 形①ありそうな, （~）しそうな ②適当な 副たぶん, おそらく

□ **limit** 名限界,《-s》範囲, 境界 動制限［限定］する

□ **limited** 動 limit（制限する）の過去, 過去分詞 形限られた, 限定の

□ **link** 名①（鎖の）輪 ②リンク ③相互［因果］関係 動連結する, つながる

□ **liquid** 名液体 形①液体（状）の, 流動する ②流ちょうな ③澄んだ ④不安定な

□ **liquidity** 名流動性, 流動資産

□ **liquidity risk** 流動性リスク

□ **list** 名名簿, 目録, 一覧表 動名簿［目録］に記入する

□ **living** 動 live（住む）の現在分詞 名生計, 生活 形①生きている, 現存の ②使用されている ③そっくりの

□ **loan** 名貸付（金）, ローン 動貸す

□ **local government** 地方自治体,

地方政府

□ **local production** 現地生産

□ **lockdown** 名ロックダウン, 封鎖 《暴動や感染病が発生したとき, 安全のために人々を建物（または特定の場所）の中に閉じ込めておくこと。また, 外部から人が入ることを禁じること》

□ **long-term** 形長期の

□ **longer** 熟 no longer もはや~でない［~しない］

□ **look back at** ~に視線を戻す, ~を振り返って見る

□ **look for** ~を探す

□ **loosen** 動①ゆるめる, ほどく ②解き放つ

□ **loss** 名①損失（額・物）, 損害, 浪費 ②失敗, 敗北

□ **Lost Decade** 失われた10年

□ **lot of** 《a~》たくさんの~

□ **low-income households** 低所得世帯

□ **low-priced** 形低価格の, 安値の

□ **lower** 形もっと低い, 下級の, 劣った 動下げる, 低くする

□ **loyal** 形忠実な, 誠実な 名忠実, 愛国者

□ **loyalty** 名忠義, 忠誠

□ **luxury** 形豪華な, 高級な, 贅沢な 名豪華さ, 贅沢（品）

M

□ **machinery** 名機械類［装置］

□ **mad** 形①気の狂った ②逆上した, 理性をなくした ③ばかげた ④（~に）熱狂［熱中］して, 夢中の

□ **made up of** 《be~》~で構成されている

□ **made-in-China** 形中国製の

□ **magnitude** 名マグニチュード《単位》

☐ **main** 形 主な, 主要な

☐ **main bank** メインバンク

☐ **main bank system** メインバンクシステム

☐ **mainly** 副 主に

☐ **mainstream** 名 主流, 本流, 大勢 形 主流の

☐ **maintain** 動 ①維持する ②養う

☐ **major** 形 ①大きいほうの, 主な, 一流の ②年長〔古参〕の 名 ①陸軍少佐 ②専攻科目 動 専攻する

☐ **major shareholder** 大株主, 主要株主

☐ **majority** 名 ①大多数, 大部分 ②過半数

☐ **make it possible for ～ to …** ～が…できるようにする

☐ **make sure that** 〔that以下を〕確認する, 確実になるようにする

☐ **make ～ into** ～を…に仕立てる

☐ **making** 動 make（作る）の現在分詞 名 制作, 製造

☐ **Malaysia** 名 マレーシア《国名》

☐ **male** 形 男の, 雄の 名 男, 雄

☐ **management** 名 ①経営, 取り扱い ②運営, 管理（側）

☐ **management position** 管理職

☐ **management system** 経営管理システム, 管理体制

☐ **manga** 名 マンガ

☐ **manner** 名 ①方法, やり方 ②態度, 様子 ③《-s》行儀, 作法, 生活様式

☐ **manufacture** 動 製造〔製作〕する 名 製造, 製作, 製品

☐ **manufacturer** 名 製造業者, メーカー

☐ **mark** 名 ①印, 記号, 跡 ②点数 ③特色 動 ①印〔記号〕をつける ②採点する ③目立たせる

☐ **marked** 動 mark（印をつける）の過去, 過去分詞 形 ①目立つ, 顕著な ②印のある, マークされた

☐ **marketing** 名 ①マーケティング ②〔市場における〕売買, 取引

☐ **mass-produce** 動 大量生産する, 量産する

☐ **mass-production** 名 大量生産

☐ **master** 名 主人, 雇い主, 師, 名匠 動 ①修得する ②～の主となる

☐ **matching** 形 調和する

☐ **material** 形 ①物質の, 肉体的な ②不可欠な, 重要な 名 材料, 原料

☐ **matter of urgency** 《a -》緊急を要する問題, 事柄

☐ **maximum** 形 最大限の, 最高の 名 最大（限）, 最高

☐ **maximum seismic intensity** 最大震度

☐ **meaning** 名 ①意味, 趣旨 ②重要性

☐ **meanwhile** 副 それまでの間, 一方では

☐ **measure** 動 ①測る, (～の)寸法がある ②評価する 名 ①寸法, 測定, 計量, 単位 ②程度, 基準

☐ **mechanism** 名 機構, 仕組み

☐ **media** 名 メディア, マスコミ, 媒体

☐ **median** 形 中央の, 中間の 名 中央分離帯

☐ **meeting** 動 meet（会う）の現在分詞 名 ①集まり, ミーティング, 面会 ②競技会

☐ **method** 名 ①方法, 手段 ②秩序, 体系

☐ **METI** 略 経済産業省（= Ministry of Economy, Trade and Industry）

☐ **Mexico** 名 メキシコ《国名》

☐ **mid-** ～半ば, ～中間の, ～中央の

☐ **middle** 名 中間, 最中 形 中間の, 中央の

☐ **Middle East** 中東

☐ **middle-aged** 形 中高年の

A
B
C
D
E
F
G
H
I
J
K
L
M
N
O
P
Q
R
S
T
U
V
W
X
Y
Z

□ **might** 助《mayの過去》①〜かもしれない ②〜してもよい、〜できる 名 力, 権力

□ **migrate** 動 移住する, 移動する, 回遊する

□ **military** 形 軍隊［軍人］の, 軍事の 名《the –》軍, 軍部

■ **Minamata Disease** 水俣病《熊本県水俣市にて公式発見された公害病》

□ **minister** 名 ①大臣, 閣僚, 公使 ②聖職者

□ **ministry** 名 ①《M-》内閣, 省庁 ②大臣の職務 ③牧師の職務

■ **Ministry of Economy, Trade and Industry** 経済産業省, METI（略）

■ **Ministry of Finance** 財務省, 大蔵省, MOF（略）

■ **Ministry of Health, Labor and Welfare** 厚生労働省, MHLW（略）

■ **Ministry of International Affairs and Communications** 総務省, MIC（略）

■ **Ministry of International Trade and Industry** 通産省, 通商産業省, MITI（略）

■ **Ministry of Land, Infrastructure, Transport and Tourism** 国土交通省, MLIT（略）

□ **minus** 前 〜を引いた 形 負の, （〜）以下の 名 不足, 欠損

□ **mire** 動 窮地［苦境］に陥らせる

□ **mismatch** 名 ミスマッチ, 不釣り合い（な組み合わせ）, 不一致

■ **MITI** 略 通産省, 通商産業省（= Ministry of International Trade and Industry）

■ **Mitsubishi** 名 三菱《日本三大財閥の一つ》

■ **Mitsui** 名 三井《日本三大財閥の一つ》

□ **model** 名 ①模型, 設計図 ②模範 形 模範の, 典型的な 動《〜をもとにして》作る, 模型を作る

■ **MOF** 略 財務省（= Ministry of Finance）

□ **mold** 名 ①型, 鋳型 ②特徴 ③かび 動 ①型に入れて作る, 形成する ②かびさせる, かびる

□ **monetary** 形 通貨の, 貨幣の, 金銭上の

□ **mood** 名 気分, 機嫌, 雰囲気, 憂うつ

□ **mood of self-restraint** 自粛ムード

□ **more** 熟 ever more これまで以上に more and more ますます

□ **motivated** 動 motivate（やる気にさせる）の過去, 過去分詞 形 やる気のある

□ **motor** 名 モーター, 発動機 動 車で行く

□ **mouretsushain** 名 猛烈社員

□ **movement** 名 ①動き, 運動 ②《-s》行動 ③引っ越し ④変動

□ **moving** 動 move（動く）の現在分詞 形 ①動いている ②感動させる

□ **much** 熟 too much 過度の

□ **multiply** 動 ①掛け算をする ②数が増える, 繁殖する

□ **myth** 名 神話

N

□ **nation** 名 国, 国家,《the –》国民

□ **national** 形 国家［国民］の, 全国の

□ **national income** 国民所得

□ **national median** 全国の中央値

□ **natural disaster** 自然災害, 天災, 不可抗力

□ **natural resource** 自然資源, 天

然資源

- □ **naturally** 副 生まれつき, 自然に, 当然

- □ **nearly** 副 ①近くに, 親しく ②ほとんど, あやうく

- □ **necessary** 形 必要な, 必然の 名 《-s》必要品, 必需品

- □ **necessity** 名 必要, 不可欠, 必要品

- □ **need to do** 〜する必要がある

- □ **NEET** 名 ニート (= Not in Education, Employment or Training)《就学・就労していない, また職業訓練も受けていない若者のこと》

- □ **negative** 形 ①否定的な, 消極的な ②負の, マイナスの, (写真が) ネガの 名 ①否定, 反対 ②ネガ, 陰画, 負数, マイナス

- □ **negligence** 名 怠慢, 不注意

- □ **negotiate** 動 交渉[協議]する

- □ **negotiation** 名 交渉, 話し合い

- □ **network** 名 回路, 網状組織, ネットワーク

- □ **new normal** ニューノーマル, 新しい生活様式

- □ **New Zealand** 名 ニュージーランド《国名》

- □ **news** 名 報道, ニュース, 便り, 知らせ

- □ **newspaper** 名 新聞 (紙)

- □ **Nikkei Stock Average** 日経平均株価

- □ **Nintendo** 名 任天堂《主に玩具やコンピュータゲームの開発・製造・販売を行う日本の企業》

- □ **Nippon Telegraph and Telephone Public Corporation** 日本電信電話公社《略称は「電電公社」, 現在の日本電信電話株式会社 (NTT) の前身》

- □ **Nixon** 名《Richard Milhous – 》ニクソン (1913–1994)《アメリカ合衆国第37代大統領》

- □ **Nixon Shock** ニクソン・ショック《米大統領のニクソンが1971年に電撃発表した, 既存の世界秩序を変革する2つの大きな方針転換のこと。1971年の中国訪問予告と翌年の米中共同宣言, 1971年の金・ドル交換の停止を指す》

- □ **no longer** もはや〜でない[〜しない]

- □ **no one** 誰も[一人も]〜ない

- □ **Nomura Institute of Capital Markets Research** 野村資本市場研究所

- □ **non-financial company** 非金融会社

- □ **non-performing loan** 不良債権

- □ **non-tariff barrier** 非関税障壁

- □ **nonetheless** 副 それでもなお, それにもかかわらず

- □ **nor** 接 〜もまたない

- □ **normal** 形 普通の, 平均の, 標準的な 名 平常, 標準, 典型

- □ **normal interest rate** 正常利子率

- □ **nosedive** 動〔株価などが〕暴落[急落]する

- □ **nothing** 代 have nothing to do with 〜と何の関係もない

- □ **novel** 形 ①新しい種類の, 新手の ②〔医〕〔ウイルスなどが〕新型の

- □ **novel coronavirus** 新型コロナウイルス

- □ **nuclear** 形 核の, 原子力の

- □ **numerical** 形 数 (字) の, 実数の

- □ **numerous** 形 多数の

- □ **nursing** 動 nurse (看病する) の現在分詞 名 看病, 育児

- □ **nurture** 動 養育する, 育てる 名 養育

O

- □ **obstruct** 動ふさぐ, 妨害する
- □ **occasional** 形時折の, まれの, 偶然の
- □ **occupation** 名①職業, 仕事, 就業 ②占有, 居住, 占領
- □ **occur** 動(事が)起こる, 生じる, (考えなどが)浮かぶ
- □ **OECD** 略経済協力開発機構 (= Organisation for Economic Co-operation and Development)
- □ **off** 熟 fall off 落ちる, 減る, 衰退する　lay off レイオフする, 一時解雇する　put off dealing with (問題)の対処を先送りにする　sell off ～を売却する
- □ **offer** 動申し出る, 申し込む, 提供する 名提案, 提供
- □ **official discount rate** 公定歩合
- □ **officially** 副公式に, 職務上, 正式に
- □ **oil** 名①油, 石油 ②油絵の具, 油絵 動油を塗る[引く], 滑らかにする
- □ **oil crisis** オイルショック, 石油危機
- □ **Okinawa** 名沖縄《地名》
- □ **Olympic** 形①オリンピックの ②《the O- games》オリンピック大会
- □ **Olympic Boom** オリンピック景気《1962年11月～1964年10月まで続いた好景気》
- □ **on (the) average** 平均して
- □ **on the increase** 増加して
- □ **on the other hand** 一方, 他方では
- □ **on the way** 途中で
- □ **on time** 時間どおりに
- □ **on top of** ～の上(部)に
- □ **once-in-a-100-year recession** 100年に一度の経済危機
- □ **one** 熟 at one time ある時には, か

つては no one 誰も[一人も]～ない one of ～の1つ[人]
- □ **ongoing** 形進行[継続・持続]している, 現在進行中の
- □ **onward** 副前方へ, 進んで 形前方への
- □ **open up** 広がる, 広げる, 開く, 開ける
- □ **opening** 動 open (開く)の現在分詞 名①開始, 始め ②開いた所, 穴 ③空き, 欠員 形開始の, 最初の, 開会の
- □ **operation** 名①操作, 作業, 動作 ②経営, 運営 ③手術 ④作戦, 軍事行動
- □ **opportunity** 名好機, 適当な時期[状況]
- □ **opposition** 名①反対 ②野党
- □ **option** 名選択(の余地), 選択可能物, 選択権
- □ **or so** ～かそこらで
- □ **order** 熟 in order to ～するために, ～しようと
- □ **organization** 名①組織(化), 編成, 団体, 機関 ②有機体, 生物
- □ **organized** 動 organize (組織する)の過去, 過去分詞 形組織化された, よくまとまった
- □ **original** 形①始めの, 元の, 本来の ②独創的な 名原型, 原文
- □ **originally** 副①元は, 元来 ②独創的に
- □ **originate** 動始まる, 始める, 起こす, 生じる
- □ **other** 熟 each other お互いに in other words すなわち, 言い換えれば on the other hand 一方, 他方では
- □ **out of** ①～から外へ, ～から抜け出して ②～から作り出して, ～を材料として ③～の範囲外に, ～から離れて ④(ある数)の中から
- □ **outflow** 名流出(すること)

□ **outlet** 名 ①出口 ②(電気の) コンセント ③直販店, 販路, アウトレット ④放送[テレビ・ラジオ]局

□ **outpost** 名 出先機関, 支店

□ **outstanding** 形 未解決の, 未払いの, 〔株式・債権などが〕発行済みの 名 未払いの負債, 貸付残高

□ **outstrip** 動 ～より勝る, ～を追い越す, ～をしのぐ

□ **over** ～ take over 引き継ぐ, 支配する, 乗っ取る

□ **overall** 形 総体的な, 全面的な 副 全般的に見れば 名 オーバーオール, 作業着

□ **overcome** 動 〔困難・障害などを〕克服する, 乗り越える, 打開する

□ **overconcentration** 名 一極集中

□ **overconcentration in Tokyo** 東京一極集中

□ **overseas** 形 海外の, 外国の 副 海外へ 名 国外

□ **overseas production** 海外生産

□ **oversight** 名 ①管理, 監視 ②不注意, 見落とし, 過失

□ **oversupply** 名 供給過剰

□ **overwhelmingly** 副 打ちのめすように, 圧倒的な力で

□ **owner-farmer system** 自作農体制

□ **ozone layer** オゾン層

P

□ **pace** 名 歩調, 速度 動 ゆっくり歩く, 行ったり来たりする

□ **package** 名 (計画・法案などの) 一括, 抱き合わせ

□ **paid-in capital** 資本金, 払込資本

□ **pandemic** 名 パンデミック《複数の国や全世界など, 広域でまん延する深刻な感染病の大流行》

□ **paralysis** 名 まひ(状態), 停滞

□ **Paris** 名 パリ《フランスの首都》

□ **Paris Agreement** 《the –》パリ協定《フランスのパリにて2015年に採択された, 気候変動抑制に関する多国間の国際的な協定》

□ **part-time** 形 パートタイムの, 非常勤の

□ **part-timer** 名 アルバイト, パートタイマー

□ **participant** 名 参加者, 出場者, 関与者

□ **participate** 動 参加する, 加わる

□ **participation** 名 参加, 関与

□ **particular** 形 ①特別の ②詳細な 名 事項, 細部, 《-s》詳細

□ **particularly** 副 特に, とりわけ

□ **partner** 名 配偶者, 仲間, 同僚 動 (～と) 組む, 提携する

□ **partnership** 名 提携, 共同経営, パートナーシップ

□ **passionate** 形 情熱的な, (感情が) 激しい, 短気な

□ **passionate salaried employees** 猛烈社員

□ **past** 形 過去の, この前の 名 過去(の出来事) 前 《時間・場所》～を過ぎて, ～を越して 副 通り越して, 過ぎて

□ **pay** 動 ①支払う, 払う, 報いる, 償う ②割に合う, ペイする 名 給料, 報い

□ **payment** 名 支払い, 払い込み

□ **peak** 名 頂点, 最高点 動 最高になる, ピークに達する

□ **pension** 名 ①年金, 恩給 ②下宿屋, ペンション 動 年金を支給する

□ **per** 前 ～につき, ～ごとに

□ **percentage** 名 パーセンテージ, 割合, 比率

□ **performance** 名 ①実行, 行為

②成績, できばえ, 業績 ③演劇, 演奏, 見世物

- □ **performance-based pay** 能力給, 成果主義に基づく賃金
- □ **period** 名①期, 期間, 時代 ②ピリオド, 終わり
- □ **permanent** 形 永続する, 永久の, 長持ちする
- □ **personal** 形①個人の, 私的な ②本人自らの
- □ **personal computer** パーソナル・コンピューター, パソコン
- □ **personal consumption** 個人消費
- □ **personnel** 名 人材, 人員, 人事課 形 職員の, 人事の
- □ **personnel cut** 人員の合理化, 人員整理 [削減]
- □ **personnel system** 人事制度 [体制・システム]
- □ **Peru** 名 ペルー《国名》
- □ **phase** 名①段階, 局面 ②側面, 様相 動 段階的に実施する
- □ **phenomenon** 名①現象, 事象 ②並はずれたもの [人]
- □ **philosophy** 名 哲学, 主義, 信条, 人生観
- □ **pick up** 再開する, 回復する
- □ **pile** 名 積み重ね, (〜の) 山 動 積み重ねる, 積もる **pile up** 積み重ねる
- □ **pioneer** 動〔ある分野の〕先駆者となる, 〔新分野などを〕開拓する, 〜に着手する
- □ **place** 熟 **put in place**《be –》〜が導入される **take place** 行われる, 起こる
- □ **placement** 名 職業紹介, 就職あっせん
- □ **plan to do** 〜するつもりである
- □ **planning** 動 plan (計画する) の現在分詞 名 立案, 開発計画
- □ **plastic product** プラスチック製品

- □ **plate** 名①(浅い) 皿, 1皿の料理 ②金属板, 標札, プレート 動 めっきする, 板金をする
- □ **player** 名①競技者, 選手, 演奏者, 俳優 ②演奏装置
- □ **Plaza Accord** プラザ合意《1985年9月22日に先進5か国 (G5) 蔵相・中央銀行総裁会議により発表された, 為替レート安定化に関する合意の通称》
- □ **plummet** 動〔価値・価格などが〕急落する, 急に下がる
- □ **plunge** 動①飛び込む, 突入する ②(ある状態に) 陥れる 名 突入, 突進
- □ **pocket calculator** 電卓
- □ **point** 熟 **from this point on** この地点から先は **turning point** 転回点, 変わり目, ターニング・ポイント
- □ **Pokémon** 名 ポケモン, ポケットモンスター《日本のゲームソフトシリーズ, および同作に登場する架空の生物, それらを題材にしたアニメなどのメディア作品の総称》
- □ **policy** 名①政策, 方針, 手段 ②保険証券
- □ **political** 形①政治の, 政党の ②策略的な
- □ **political issue** 政治問題
- □ **pollution-related** 形 公害に関連した
- □ **population** 名 人口, 住民 (数)
- □ **pose** 動〔問題などを〕引き起こす, もたらす, 〔負担を〕課す
- □ **position** 名①位置, 場所, 姿勢 ②地位, 身分, 職 ③立場, 状況 動 置く, 配置する
- □ **positive** 形①前向きな, 肯定的な, 好意的な ②明確な, 明白な, 確信している ③プラスの 名①正数, プラス, 陽極 ②ポジ, 陽画
- □ **possibility** 名 可能性, 見込み, 将来性

□ **possible** 形 ①可能な ②ありうる, 起こりうる **as ～ as possible** できるだけ～ **make it possible for ～ to …** ～が…できるようにする

□ **post-bubble low** 《株》バブル (崩壊) 後の底値 [最安値]

□ **postpone** 動 延期する

□ **postwar** 形 戦後の

□ **postwar reconstruction** 戦後復興

□ **potential** 形 可能性がある, 潜在的な 名 可能性, 潜在能力

□ **poverty** 名 貧乏, 貧困, 欠乏, 不足

□ **power** 熟 **take back power** 権力を取り戻す

□ **powerful** 形 力強い, 実力のある, 影響力のある

□ **pre-industrial** 形 産業革命前の

□ **pre-planned** 形 あらかじめ計画 [用意] された

□ **precision equipment** 精密機器

□ **predict** 動 予測 [予想] する

□ **prefer** 動 (～のほうを) 好む, (～のほうが) よいと思う

□ **premiership** 名 首相の任期 [職・地位・任務]

□ **premium** 名 ①保険料, 保険の掛け金 ②奨励金 ③割り増し (料金)

□ **present** 熟 **at present** 今のところ, 現在は, 目下

□ **preserve** 動 保存 [保護] する, 保つ

□ **president** 名 ①大統領 ②社長, 学長, 頭取

□ **pressure** 名 プレッシャー, 圧力, 圧縮, 重荷 動 圧力をかける

□ **prevalent** 形 広く行き渡った, 優勢な

□ **prewar** 形 戦前の 副 戦前に

□ **price** 名 ①値段, 価格 ②《-s》物価, 相場 動 値段をつける, 値段を聞く

□ **price destruction** 価格破壊

□ **price war** 値下げ競争, 価格競争

□ **primary** 形 第一の, 主要な, 最初の, 初期の 名 ①第一のこと ②予備選挙

□ **prime** 形 第一の, 最も重要な 名 《the [one's] –》全盛期

□ **prime minister** 首相, 〔日本の〕内閣総理大臣

□ **principal** 形 主な, 第一の, 主要な, 重要な 名 ①長, 社長, 校長 ②主役, 主犯, 本人

□ **prior** 形 (時間・順序が) 前の, (～に) 優先する, (～より) 重要な

□ **priority** 名 優先 (すること), 優先度 [順位]

□ **Priority Production System** 傾斜生産方式

□ **private** 形 ①私的な, 個人の ②民間の, 私立の ③内密の, 人里離れた

□ **private sector** 民間企業 [部門]

□ **private-sector** 形 私営の, 民営の

□ **private-sector investment** 民間投資

□ **privatization** 名 民営化

□ **privatize** 動 民営化する, 私有化する

□ **proactive** 形 〔行動などが〕先を見越した, 先回りした, 積極的な, 前向きな

□ **proceed** 動 進む, 進展する, 続ける 名 《-s》①結果 ②収益, 所得, 売却代金

□ **process** 名 ①過程, 経過, 進行 ②手順, 方法, 製法, 加工

□ **processing trade** 加工貿易

□ **procure** 動 〔入手困難な物を〕入手 [調達・獲得] する

□ **product** 名 ①製品, 産物 ②成果, 結果

□ **production** 名 製造, 生産

□ **production management system** 生産管理システム

□ **production process** 生産工程

□ **production system** 生産システム

□ **production-unit term** 生産台数の単位[項目]

□ **productive** 形生産的な, 豊富な

□ **productivity** 名生産性

□ **professional** 形専門の, プロの, 職業的な 名専門家, プロ

□ **profit** 名利益, 利潤, ため 動利益になる, (人の)ためになる, 役立つ

□ **profitability** 名収益性, 利益性

□ **progress** 名①進歩, 前進 ②成り行き, 経過 動前進する, 上達する

□ **prolonged** 形長引く, 長期の

□ **promote** 動促進する, 昇進[昇級]させる

□ **promotion** 名①昇進 ②促進 ③宣伝販売

□ **property** 名①財産, 所有物[地] ②性質, 属性

□ **proportion** 名①割合, 比率, 分け前 ②釣り合い, 比例

□ **protective** 形保護する, 保護(用)の 名保護するもの

□ **protocol** 名①外交儀礼, 議定書 ②(データ通信での)プロトコル

□ **prove** 動①証明する ②(〜である ことが)わかる, (〜と)なる

□ **provide** 動①供給する, 用意する, (〜に)備える ②規定する

□ **provided** 動provide(供給する) の過去, 過去分詞 接もし〜ならば, 仮に〜とすれば

□ **provider** 名供給する人, 供給者, 調達者

□ **province** 名①州, 省 ②地方, 田舎 ③範囲, 領域

□ **provoke** 動①怒らせる ②刺激して〜させる ③引き起こす

□ **public** 名一般の人々, 大衆 形公の, 公開の

□ **publish** 動①発表[公表]する ②出版[発行]する

□ **purely** 副まったくの, 単に, 純粋に

□ **pursue** 動①追う, つきまとう ②追求する, 従事する

□ **push down** 押し倒す

□ **put in place** 《be – 》〜が導入される

□ **put in simple terms** 簡単な言い方をすれば

□ **put off dealing with** (問題)の対処を先送りにする

Q

□ **qualitative** 形質的な, 性質(上)の

□ **quality** 名①質, 性質, 品質 ②特性 ③良質

□ **quantitative** 形量の, 量的な, 量に関する

□ **quantitative and qualitative financial easing** 量的・質的金融緩和

□ **quantity** 名①量 ②《-ties》多量, たくさん

□ **quarter** 名①4分の1, 25セント, 15分, 3カ月 ②方面, 地域 ③部署 動4等分する

□ **quickly** 副敏速に, 急いで

□ **quit** 動やめる, 辞職する, 中止する

R

□ **R&D** 略研究開発(= research and development)

□ **radio** 名①ラジオ ②無線電話[電報] 動放送する

□ **raid** 名急襲, (警察の)手入れ 動急襲する, 手入れする

- [ ] **raise** 動①上げる, 高める ②起こす ③～を育てる ④（資金を）調達する 名高める［上げる］こと, 昇給

- [ ] **range** 名列, 連なり, 範囲 動①並ぶ, 並べる ②およぶ

- [ ] **rank** 名①列 ②階級, 位 動①並ぶ, 並べる ②分類する

- [ ] **rapid** 形速い, 急な, すばやい 名《-s》急流, 早瀬

- [ ] **rapid economic growth** 高度経済成長

- [ ] **rapidly** 副速く, 急速, すばやく, 迅速に

- [ ] **rate** 名①割合, 率 ②相場, 料金 動①見積もる, 評価する［される］②等級をつける

- [ ] **rate of real economic growth** 実質経済成長率

- [ ] **ratio** 名割合, 比率, 率, 歩合, 比例

- [ ] **ration** 名〔原材料・資源などの一定量を〕分配［配給］する, 割り当てる

- [ ] **ravage** 動①破壊（行為）②《the－s》損害, 惨害, 痛ましいほどの被害

- [ ] **raw** 形①生の, 未加工の ②未熟な 名生もの

- [ ] **raw material** 原材料, 原料, 素材

- [ ] **reading** 動 read（読む）の現在分詞 名読書, 読み物, 朗読

- [ ] **real estate** 不動産, 土地

- [ ] **real GDP** 実質GDP

- [ ] **realignment** 名再編, 再調整, 再編成

- [ ] **receipt** 名受領書, 受け取ること, レシート

- [ ] **recent** 形近ごろの, 近代の

- [ ] **recently** 副近ごろ, 最近

- [ ] **recession** 名景気後退, 不況, 後退

- [ ] **reckon** 動①数える ②（～と）みなす, 推測する

- [ ] **recognition** 名承認, 表彰, お礼

- [ ] **recognize** 動認める, 認識［承認］する

- [ ] **reconstruction** 名再建, 復興, 復元

- [ ] **reconstruction bond** 復興債

- [ ] **recover** 動①取り戻す, ばん回する ②回復する

- [ ] **recovery** 名回復, 復旧, 立ち直り

- [ ] **rectify** 動①〔誤りなどを〕正す, 修正する, 改正する ②〔違反などを〕是正する

- [ ] **redemption** 名償還, 買い戻し, 弁済

- [ ] **reduce** 動①減じる ②しいて～させる, （～の）状態にする

- [ ] **reduction** 名①下げること, 減少, 値下げ, 割引 ②縮図 ③換算, 約分, 還元

- [ ] **reexamine** 動再検査する, もう一度調べる, 見直す

- [ ] **refer** 動①《－to～》～に言及する, ～と呼ぶ ②～を参照する, ～に問い合わせる

- [ ] **reform** 動改善する, 改革する 名改善, 改良

- [ ] **refrigerator** 名冷蔵庫

- [ ] **regard** 動①（～を…と）見なす ②尊敬する, 重きを置く ③関係がある **regarded as**《be－》～と見なされる 名①注意, 関心 ②尊敬, 好感 ③《-s》（手紙などで）よろしくというあいさつ

- [ ] **region** 名①地方, 地域 ②範囲

- [ ] **regional** 形地方の, 局地的な

- [ ] **regional revitalization** 地方創生

- [ ] **register** 動～を正式に記録［登録］する, 記名する

- [ ] **regulation** 名規則, 規定, 規制

- [ ] **rein** 名手綱, 拘束, 統制, 統御力, 支配権, 指揮権 動手綱で御する, 制御する, 制止する

- [ ] **reinforce** 動補強［強化］する, 拍車をかける

- [ ] **relation** 名①（利害）関係, 間柄

123

②親戚

□ **relationship** 图関係, 関連, 血縁関係

□ **relative** 形関係のある, 相対的な 图親戚, 同族

□ **relative income poverty** 相対的貧困

□ **relatively** 副比較的, 相対的に

□ **relaxed** 動relax（くつろがせる）の過去, 過去分詞 形①くつろいだ, ゆったりした ②ざっくばらんな

□ **release** 動①解き放す, 釈放する ②免除する ③発表する, リリースする 图解放, 釈放

□ **remain** 動①残っている, 残る ②（～の）ままである[いる] 图《-s》①残り（もの）②遺跡

□ **remaining** 動remain（残っている）の現在分詞 形残った, 残りの

□ **remove** 動①取り去る, 除去する ②（衣類を）脱ぐ

□ **rename** 動新しい名前をつける, 改名する

□ **renewed** 動renew（新しくする）過去, 過去分詞 形更新した, 回復した

□ **renovation** 图①革新, 刷新 ②修理, 修繕 ③元気回復

□ **reorganize** 動再編成する, 再組織する

□ **repay** 動①払い戻す, 返金する ②報いる, 恩返しする

□ **repayment** 图払い戻し, 返済

□ **repeated** 動repeat（繰り返す）の過去, 過去分詞 形繰り返された, 度重なる

□ **replace** 動①取り替える, 差し替える ②元に戻す

□ **reportedly** 副報道[伝えられるところ]によると

□ **represent** 動①表現する ②意味する ③代表する

□ **request** 图願い, 要求（物）, 需要

at the request of ～の要請により, ～の要求に応じて 動求める, 申し込む

□ **require** 動①必要とする, 要する ②命じる, 請求する

□ **rescue** 動救う 图救助, 救出

□ **research** 图調査, 研究 動調査する, 研究する

□ **reserve** 動①とっておく, 備えておく ②予約する ③留保する 图①蓄え, 備え ②準備[積立]金 ③遠慮 形予備の

□ **resource** 图①資源, 財産 ②手段, 方策

□ **respectively** 副それぞれに, めいめい

□ **respond** 動答える, 返答[応答]する

□ **response** 图応答, 反応, 返答

□ **restore** 動元に戻す, 復活させる

□ **restrict** 動制限する, 禁止する

□ **restricted** 動restrict（制限する）の過去, 過去分詞 形制限された, 限られた

□ **restriction** 图制限, 規制

□ **restructuring** 動restructure（再編成する）の現在分詞 图リストラ, 構造改革, 再構築

□ **result** 图結果, 成り行き, 成績 **as a result** その結果（として）**as a result of** ～の結果（として）動（結果として）起こる, 生じる, 結局～になる

□ **resume** 動再び始める, 再開する

□ **retail** 形小売りの 图小売り（店）

□ **retain** 動①保つ, 持ち続ける ②覚えている

□ **retirement** 图引退, （定年）退職 **early retirement** 早期退職

□ **return of Okinawa to Japan** 沖縄返還

□ **revenue** 图所得, 収入, 利益, （国の）歳入

☐ **revitalization** 名 再生, 再活性化, 回復

☐ **revitalize** 動 ～を活性化する, ～を再生する, ～を復興させる

☐ **revival** 名 復活, 再生, リバイバル

☐ **revive** 動 生き返る, 生き返らせる, 復活する[させる]

☐ **rid** 動 取り除く **get rid of** ～を取り除く

☐ **ripple** 名 さざ波(のような音), 波状(の動き), 波紋, ざわめき 動 さざ波を立てる, さざ波が立つ, 波紋を起こす

☐ **risen** 動 rise (昇る)の過去分詞 形 上がった, 起こった

☐ **rising** 形 昇る, 高まる

☐ **risk** 名 危険 動 危険にさらす, 賭ける, 危険をおかす

☐ **road** 熟 **set on the road to** ～への軌道に乗せる

☐ **role** 名 ①(劇などの)役 ②役割, 任務 **leading role** 主導的役割 **take a leading role in** ～で主導的役割を担う[果たす] **take on the role of** ～の役割を引き受ける

☐ **roll** 動 ①転がる, 転がす ②(波などが)うねる, 横揺れする ③(時が)たつ **roll out** 展開する, 広げる 名 ①一巻き ②名簿, 目録

☐ **rolling blackout** 計画停電, 輪番停電

☐ **root** 名 ①根, 根元 ②根源, 原因 ③《-s》先祖, ルーツ 動 根づかせる, 根づく

☐ **roughly** 副 ①おおよそ, 概略的に, 大ざっぱに ②手荒く, 粗雑に

☐ **ruin** 名 破滅, 滅亡, 破産, 廃墟 動 破滅させる

☐ **Ryutaro Hashimoto** 橋本龍太郎 (1937-2006)《第82・83代内閣総理大臣》

S

☐ **sacred** 形 神聖な, 厳粛な

☐ **salary** 名 給料

☐ **sale** 名 販売, 取引, 大売り出し

☐ **sales weapon** 販売の武器

☐ **saving** 動 save (救う)の現在分詞 名 ①節約 ②《-s》貯金 ③救助

☐ **savings rate** 貯蓄率

☐ **scale** 名 ①目盛り ②規模, 割合, 程度, スケール ③うろこ(鱗) ④てんびん, はかり 動 はかりにかける, はかる

☐ **scene** 熟 **come on the scene** 登場する, 姿を現す

☐ **scientific** 形 科学の, 科学的な

☐ **Second Oil Crisis** 第二次石油危機

☐ **secondly** 副 第2に, 次に

☐ **section chief** 課長

☐ **sector** 名 ①(産業などの)部門, セクター ②(幾何で)扇形

☐ **secure** 形 ①安全な ②しっかりした, 保証された 動 ①安全にする ②確保する, 手に入れる

☐ **security** 名 ①安全(性), 安心 ②担保, 抵当 《-ties》有価証券

☐ **seek** 動 捜し求める, 求める

☐ **seem** 動 (～に)見える, (～のように)思われる

☐ **seen as** 《be -》～として見られる

☐ **seismic** 形 地震の[に関する・によって引き起こされる]

☐ **seldom** 副 まれに, めったに～ない

☐ **self-assessment** 名 自己査定[評価]

☐ **self-defense** 名 自衛, 自己防衛, 正当防衛

☐ **self-restraint** 名 自制, 自粛

☐ **sell off** ～を売却する

☐ **semiconductor** 名 半導体

A
B
C
D
E
F
G
H
I
J
K
L
M
N
O
P
Q
R
S
T
U
V
W
X
Y
Z

- **senior** 形 年長の，年上の，古参の，上級の　名 年長者，先輩，先任者
- **seniority** 名 年功序列，年長
- **seniority system** 年功序列制度
- **sense** 名 ①感覚，感じ ②〈-s〉意識，正気，本性 ③常識，分別，センス ④意味　動 感じる，気づく
- **series** 名 一続き，連続，シリーズ
- **serious** 形 ①まじめな，真剣な ②重大な，深刻な，(病気などが)重い
- **seriousness** 名 まじめ，真剣，深刻
- **serve** 動 ①仕える，奉仕する ②(客の)応対をする，給仕する，食事[飲み物]を出す ③(役目を)果たす，務める，役に立つ
- **service** 名 ①勤務，業務 ②公益事業 ③点検，修理 ④奉仕，貢献　動 保守点検する，(点検)修理をする
- **set for ~ to ...** ～が…する準備を整える
- **set on the road to** ～への軌道に乗せる
- **set up** 配置する，セットする，設置する
- **settled** 動 settle (安定する)の過去，過去分詞　形 固定した，落ち着いた，解決した
- **severe** 形 厳しい，深刻な，激しい
- **shake** 動 ①振る，揺れる，揺さぶる，震える ②動揺させる　名 振ること
- **shape** 名 ①形，姿，型 ②状態，調子　動 形づくる，具体化する
- **shareholder** 名 株主
- **shareholding** 名 株式保有
- **sharp** 形 ①鋭い，とがった ②刺すような，きつい ③鋭敏な ④急な　副 ①鋭く，急に ②(時間が)ちょうど
- **sheet** 名 ①シーツ ②(紙などの)1枚
- **shift** 動 移す，変える，転嫁する　名 ①変化，移動 ②交替，(交代制の)勤務(時間)，シフト
- **shifted** 動 shift (動く，方向を変える)の過去形
- **Shinzo Abe** 安倍晋三 (1954–)《第90・96～98代内閣総理大臣》
- **shipbuilding** 名 造船
- **shoot up** 急上昇する，〔株価などが〕急騰する
- **shortage** 名 不足，欠乏
- **shrank** 動 shrink (縮む)の過去
- **shrink** 動 ①縮む，縮小する ②尻込みする，ひるむ
- **shut** 動 ①閉まる，閉める，閉じる ②たたむ ③閉じ込める ④shutの過去，過去分詞
- **side** 名 ①側，横，そば，斜面　形 ①側面の，横の ②副次的な　動 (～の)側につく，賛成する
- **signatory** 形 調印[署名・加盟]した　名 ①調印者，署名者 ②調印国 (= signatory country)
- **signatory country** 〔条約などの〕調印国，署名国，加盟国
- **significant** 形 ①重要な，有意義な ②大幅な，著しい ③意味ありげな
- **significantly** 副 ①意味深長に，意味ありげに ②著しく，かなり
- **SII** 略 日米構造協議 (= Structural Impediments Initiative)
- **silent** 形 ①無言の，黙っている ②静かな，音を立てない ③活動しない
- **silent shareholder** 物言わぬ株主，サイレント株主
- **similar** 形 同じような，類似した，相似の
- **simple** 熟 put in simple terms 簡単な言い方をすれば
- **since** 熟 ever since それ以来ずっと
- **Singapore** 名 シンガポール《国名》
- **single** 形 ①たった1つの ②1人用

の，それぞれの ③独身の ④片道の

□ **single-parent household** ひ
とり親世帯

□ **situation** 名①場所，位置 ②状況，
境遇，立場

□ **skill** 名①技能，技術 ②上手，熟練

□ **slip** 動滑る，滑らせる，滑って転ぶ
名滑ること

□ **slogan** 名スローガン，モットー

□ **slowdown** 名①〔景気の〕後退，
低迷，減速 ②サボタージュ，怠業

□ **slowly** 副遅く，ゆっくり

□ **slump** 名①不振 ②急落，暴落 ③
不況 動①スランプに陥る ②衰える
③（物価などが）暴落する

□ **small** in small steps 少しずつ，
だんだんと

□ **smaller government** 小さな
政府

□ **so** 熟 and so そこで，それだから，
それで or so ～かそこらで so ～
that … 非常に～なので…

□ **so-called** 形いわゆる，～といわ
れて

□ **soar** 動高く飛ぶ，舞い上がる，急騰
する，高くそびえる

□ **social** 形①社会の，社会的な ②社
交的な，愛想のよい

□ **social problem** 社会問題

□ **social security system
[program]** 社会保障制度

□ **socially isolated** 《be－》社会的
に孤立している

□ **society** 名社会，世間

□ **socio-economic system** 社
会経済システム［体制］

□ **software** 名ソフト（ウェア）

□ **sole** 形唯一の，単独の 名足の裏，
靴底

□ **solve** 動解く，解決する

□ **someone** 代ある人，誰か It is ～
for someone to … （人）が…するの

は～だ get someone to volunteer
for（人に）～を志願させる

□ **something** 代①ある物，何か ②
いくぶん，多少

□ **sometimes** 副時々，時たま

□ **somewhere** 副①どこかへ［に］
②いつか，およそ

□ **Sony Computer
Entertainment** 株式会社ソニー
・コンピュータエンタテインメント
《現在の株式会社ソニー・インタラク
ティブエンタテインメントの前身》

□ **Sony Walkman** ソニー・ウォー
クマン《ポータブルオーディオプレイ
ヤーの商品名》

□ **sophisticated** 形①洗練された，
都会的な ②世慣れた，上品ぶった

□ **sort** 名種類，品質 sort of《a－》～
のようなもの，一種の～ 動分類する

□ **sought** 動seek（捜し求める）の過
去，過去分詞

□ **source** 名源，原因，もと

□ **southeast** 名南東(部) 形南東の，
南東向きの 副南東へ，南東から

□ **Southeast Asia** 東南アジア

□ **spearhead** 動〔活動・攻撃などの〕
先頭に立つ，陣頭指揮を執る

□ **special deficit-financing
bond** 特例公債

□ **special zones for structural
reform** 構造改革特区

□ **specific** 形明確な，はっきりした，
具体的な

□ **specifically** 副特に，明確に，具体
的に

□ **speculative** 形①思索的な，思惑
の ②投機的な speculative fever 投
機熱

□ **speed** 名速力，速度 動①急ぐ，急
がせる ②制限速度以上で走る，スピ
ード違反をする

□ **spiral** 名らせん 形らせん状の，渦
巻き型の 動らせん形になる

- □ **spirit** 名①霊 ②精神, 気力
- □ **Spirited Away** 千と千尋の神隠し《2001年公開の長編アニメーション映画。監督は宮崎駿》
- □ **spur** 名拍車 動拍車をかける, 駆り立てる
- □ **stability** 名安定(性), 持続
- □ **stabilize** 動安定する, 固定する
- □ **stable** 形安定した, 堅固な, 分解しにくい 名馬小屋, 厩舎
- □ **staff** 名職員, スタッフ 動配置する
- □ **staffer** 名スタッフ, 職員, 部員, 社員
- □ **stage** 名①舞台 ②段階 動上演する
- □ **stagnant** 形よどんだ, 流れない
- □ **stagnate** 動①停滞する, 活気がなくなる ②〔流れなどが〕よどむ
- □ **stagnation** 名停滞, 低迷, 不振
- □ **standard** 名標準, 規格, 規準 形①標準の ②一流の, 優秀な
- □ **standstill** 名〔動きや行為の完全な〕停止, 休止
- □ **start doing** ～し始める
- □ **start to do** ～し始める
- □ **state** 名①あり様, 状態 ②国家, (アメリカなどの)州 ③階層, 地位 動述べる, 表明する
- □ **statement** 名声明, 述べること
- □ **statistic** 名統計値, 統計量
- □ **stay at** (場所)にとどまる
- □ **stay at home** 家にこもる, 国内にとどまる
- □ **stay away from** ～から離れている
- □ **stay with** ～の所にとどまる
- □ **stay-at-home mother** 専業主婦
- □ **steadily** 副しっかりと
- □ **steady** 形①しっかりした, 安定した, 落ち着いた ②堅実な, まじめな

- □ **steamroller** 動強圧的[強引]に押し通す[押し切る], 圧勝する
- □ **steel** 名鋼, 鋼鉄(製の物) 形鋼鉄の, 堅い
- □ **steps** 熟 in small steps 少しずつ, だんだんと
- □ **stimulate** 動①刺激する ②促す, 活性化させる ③元気づける
- □ **stimulus** 名刺激(物), 激励
- □ **stock** 名①貯蔵 ②仕入れ品, 在庫品 ③株式 動仕入れる, 蓄える
- □ **stock price** 株価
- □ **stockbroking** 名株式仲買, 証券会社
- □ **stop doing** ～するのをやめる
- □ **strategic** 形戦略的な, 戦略上の
- □ **strategically** 副戦略的に
- □ **strategy** 名戦略, 作戦, 方針
- □ **streamlining** 名合理化 形合理化の(ための)
- □ **strength** 名①力, 体力 ②長所, 強み ③強度, 濃度
- □ **strengthen** 動強くする, しっかりさせる
- □ **strengthening** 名強化
- □ **strict** 形厳しい, 厳密な
- □ **strong dollar** 《経済》ドル高
- □ **strong yen** 《経済》円高
- □ **strong-yen recession** 円高不況
- □ **strongly** 副強く, 頑丈に, 猛烈に, 熱心に
- □ **strove** 動 strive (努める)の過去
- □ **struck** 動 strike (打つ)の過去, 過去分詞
- □ **structural** 形構造(上)の
- □ **Structural Impediments Initiative (SII)** 日米構造協議
- □ **structural reform** 構造改革
- □ **structure** 名構造, 骨組み, 仕組み 動組織立てる

128

□ **style** 名やり方, 流儀, 様式, スタイル

□ **subcontractor** 名下請業者, 請負業者, 再委託先

□ **subdued** 形①〔活動などが予想よりも〕不活発な, 静かな ②〔光・色・音などが通常よりも〕抑えられた

□ **subprime loan** サブプライムローン《信用度の低い顧客に高金利で貸し出す融資》

□ **subsequently** 副その後, それに続いて

□ **subsidiary** 名①子会社, 関連子会社 ②付属(物) 形①従属的な, 従属する ②補助的な, 補助的な ③助成金による

□ **subsidiary company** 子会社, 系列会社

□ **subsidy** 名助成金, 補助金

□ **success** 名成功, 幸運, 上首尾

□ **successful** 形成功した, うまくいった

□ **successfully** 副首尾よく, うまく

□ **successor** 名後継者, 相続人, 後任者

□ **such as** たとえば~, ~のような

□ **such ～ as …** …のような~

□ **sudden** 形突然の, 急な

□ **suffer** 動①(苦痛・損害などを)受ける, こうむる ②(病気に)なる, 苦しむ, 悩む

□ **suffering** 動suffer(受ける)の現在分詞 名苦痛, 苦しみ, 苦難

□ **sufficient** 形十分な, 足りる

□ **suggest** 動①提案する ②示唆する

□ **suit** 名①スーツ, 背広 ②訴訟 ③ひとそろい, 一組 動①適合する[させる] ②似合う

□ **suitable** 形適当な, 似合う, ふさわしい

□ **sum** 名①総計 ②金額 動①合計する ②要約する

□ **supermarket** 名スーパーマーケット

□ **superpower** 名超大国, 強国, 異常な力

□ **supplier** 名供給者, 供給業者, 納入業者

□ **supply** 動供給[配給]する, 補充する 名供給(品), 給与, 補充

□ **supply chain** サプライチェーン《製品が原材料の調達から, 生産・物流・販売を経て, 消費者の手に届くまでの全過程》

□ **support** 動①支える, 支持する ②養う, 援助する 名①支え, 支持 ②援助, 扶養

□ **sure** 熟 **make sure that**〔that以下〕を確認する, 確実になるようにする

□ **surge** 名①大波 ②(感情などの)高まり ③急上昇 動(波のように)押し寄せる, 沸き上がる

□ **surpass** 動勝る, しのぐ

□ **surplus** 名余り, 残り, 余分, 余剰, 黒字 形余った, 過剰の, 黒字の

□ **survive** 動①生き残る, 存続する, なんとかなる ②長生きする, 切り抜ける

□ **suspension** 名①つるす[ぶら下げる]こと ②〔一時的な〕停止, 保留, 差し止め

□ **switch** 名スイッチ 動①スイッチを入れる[切る] ②切り替える, 切り替わる

T

□ **take a leading role in** ～で主導的役割を担う[果たす]

□ **take back power** 権力を取り戻す

□ **take care of** ～の世話をする, ～の面倒を見る, ～を管理する

□ **take on the role of** ～の役割を引き受ける

□ **take over** 引き継ぐ, 支配する, 乗っ取る

□ **take place** 行われる, 起こる

□ **take ～ for granted** ～を当然のことと思う

□ **takeover** 名 ①〔権力や支配権の力ずくの〕獲得, 奪取 ②企業買収

□ **tangible** 形 実体のある, 現実の

□ **target** 名 標的, 目的物, 対象 動 的[目標]にする

□ **tariff** 名 関税(率)

□ **tariff reduction** 関税引き下げ

□ **tax** 名 ①税 ②重荷, 重い負担 動 ①課税する ②重荷を負わせる

□ **tax code** 税法

□ **tax receipts** 租税収入

□ **tax revenue** 税収, 歳入

□ **tax sources** 税源

□ **taxation** 名 課税, 徴税

□ **teamwork** 名 チームワーク, 共同作業

□ **technological** 名 技術上の, (科学)技術の

□ **technological innovation** 技術革新

□ **technologically** 副 技術的に

□ **technology** 名 テクノロジー, 科学技術

■ **Teito Rapid Transit Authority** 帝都高速度交通営団, 営団地下鉄《日本政府および東京都が出資していた東京23区の地下鉄事業者。1941年～2004年まで存在していた》

□ **telegraph** 名 電報, 電信 動 電報を打つ

□ **television** 名 テレビ

□ **telework** 名 テレワーク, 在宅勤務の仕事

□ **temp** 名 臨時職員, 期間限定社員

動 派遣社員[臨時職員]として働く

□ **temp staffer** 派遣社員, 派遣職員

□ **temp worker** 臨時[非正規]雇用者

□ **temperature** 名 温度, 体温

□ **temporarily** 副 一時的に, 仮に, 当面は

□ **temporary** 形 一時的な, 仮の

□ **tend** ①(～の)傾向がある, (～)しがちである ②面倒を見る, 手入れをする

□ **TEPCO** 略 東京電力株式会社 (= Tokyo Electric Power Co., Inc.)

□ **term** 名 ①期間, 期限 ②語, 用語 ③⟨-s⟩条件 ④⟨-s⟩関係, 仲

□ **termination** 名 終了, 結末

□ **terms** 熟 in terms of ～の言葉で言えば, ～の点から put in simple terms 簡単な言い方をすれば

□ **territorial** 形 領土の, 領土に関する, 土地の

□ **textile** 名 布地, 織物, 繊維製品 形 織物の

□ **textile industry** 繊維産業

□ **thanks to** ～のおかげで, ～の結果

□ **that** 熟 make sure that〔that以下〕を確認する, 確実になるようにする so ～ that … 非常に～なので…

□ **theory** 名 理論, 学説

□ **therefore** 副 したがって, それゆえ, その結果

□ **thirdly** 副〔要点などを説明する順序として〕第三に, 3番目に

□ **this** 熟 from this point on この地点から先は in this way このようにして like this このような, こんなふうに

□ **though** 接 ①～にもかかわらず, ～だが ②たとえ～でも 副 しかし

□ **three arrows** (アベノミクス)3本の矢

130

□ **three Cs** 新・三種の神器《1960年代半ばに普及した3種類の耐久消費財。カラーテレビ（Color television）・クーラー（Cooler）・自動車（Car）》

□ **three excesses** 3つの過剰

□ **three new sacred treasures** 新・三種の神器《1960年代半ばに普及した3種類の耐久消費財。カラーテレビ（Color television）・クーラー（Cooler）・自動車（Car）》

□ **three sacred treasures** 三種の神器《1950年代後半に普及した3種類の耐久消費財。白黒テレビ・洗濯機・冷蔵庫》

□ **through** 熟 break through 〜を打ち破る go through 通り抜ける，一つずつ順番に検討する

□ **thus** 副 ①このように ②これだけ ③かくして，だから

□ **tight** 形 堅い，きつい，ぴんと張った 副 堅く，しっかりと

□ **tight-money policy** 金融引締め政策

□ **time** 熟 at one time ある時には，かつては for the first time 初めて on time 時間どおりに

□ **tobacco** 名 たばこ

□ **Tohoku region** 東北地方《地域名》

□ **Tokaido bullet train** 東海道新幹線

□ **Tokyo** 名 東京《地名》

□ **Tokyo (foreign exchange) market** 東京外国為替市場

□ **Tokyo Electric Power Company (TEPCO)** 東京電力株式会社

□ **Tokyo Metro** 東京メトロ《東京地下鉄株式会社の愛称》

□ **too much** 過度の

□ **tool** 名 道具，用具，工具

□ **top** 熟 on top of 〜の上（部）に

□ **topic** 名 話題，見出し

□ **torrential exports** 集中豪雨的輸出

□ **total** 形 総計の，全体の，完全な 名 全体，合計 動 合計する

□ **total trade** 貿易総額

□ **totally** 副 全体的に，すっかり

□ **touchpoint** 名 接点，タッチポイント

□ **tough** 形 堅い，丈夫な，たくましい，骨の折れる，困難な

□ **tourism** 名 ①観光旅行，観光業 ②《集合的》観光客

□ **tourist** 名 旅行者，観光客

□ **toxic** 形 毒性のある，有毒な

□ **Toyota Motor** トヨタ自動車株式会社《世界有数の大手自動車メーカー》

□ **TPP-11** 名 環太平洋パートナーシップに関する包括的及び先進的な協定《2018年に日本を含む11の国々によって締結された多国間貿易協定》

□ **trade** 名 取引，貿易，商業 動 取引する，貿易する，商売する

□ **trade deficit** 貿易赤字

□ **trade friction** 貿易摩擦

□ **trade liberalization** 貿易自由化

□ **trade problem** 貿易問題

□ **trade surplus** 輸出超過額

□ **trading** 名 貿易，通商，商取引

□ **trading partner** 貿易相手国

□ **traditional** 形 伝統的な

□ **training** 動 train（訓練する）の現在分詞 名 ①トレーニング，訓練 ②コンディション，体調

□ **Trans-Pacific Partnership (TPP)** 環太平洋パートナーシップ協定《2016年に日本を含む12の国々の間で署名された経済連携協定（EPA）》

□ **transfer** 動 ①移動する ②移す ③譲渡する 名 ①移動，移送 ②譲渡 ③乗り換え

☐ **transit** 名通過, 乗り換え, トランジット

☐ **transparent** 形 ①透明な, 透けて見える ②わかりやすい

☐ **transport** 動輸送[運送]する 名輸送, 運送(機関)

☐ **transportation machinery** 輸送用機械

☐ **travel agency** 旅行代理店

☐ **treasure** 名財宝, 貴重品, 宝物 動秘蔵する

☐ **tremendous** 形すさまじい, とても大きい

☐ **trend** 名トレンド, 傾向

☐ **trendsetter** 名流行をつくる人

☐ **tried** 動try(試みる)の過去, 過去分詞 形試験済みの, 信頼できる

☐ **trigger** 名引き金, きっかけ, 要因

☐ **trillion** 名1兆

☐ **triple** 名 ①3倍(の数) ②三塁打 形3倍の, 3重の, 3種類の 動3倍になる[する], 3重になる

☐ **triple reform** 三位一体の改革

☐ **truck** 名トラック, 運搬車 動トラックで運ぶ

☐ **Trump** 名《Donald John –》トランプ(1946–)《アメリカ合衆国第45代大統領》

☐ **trust** 動信用[信頼]する, 委託する 名信用, 信頼, 委託

☐ **trying** 動try(やってみる)の現在分詞 形つらい, 苦しい, しゃくにさわる

☐ **tsunami** 名津波

☐ **turn** 熟 **in turn** 順番に, 立ち代わって

☐ **turning** 動turn(ひっくり返す)の現在分詞 名回転, 曲がり角 **turning point** 転回点, 変わり目, ターニング・ポイント

☐ **2008 Financial Crisis**《the –》2008年の金融危機《2007年に顕在化

したサブプライム住宅ローン危機を発端としたリーマン・ショックと, それに連鎖して2008年に発生した一連の国際的な金融危機》

U

☐ **U.S.** 略《the –》アメリカ合衆国(= United States of America)

☐ **U.S. government bond** 米国債

☐ **U.S.-Japan Structural Impediments Initiative** 日米構造協議

☐ **unable** 形《be – to ~》~することができない

☐ **unchecked** 形〔悪い事などが〕歯止め[抑制]が利かない

☐ **undeniable** 形明白な, 否定しようがない

☐ **underline** 動下線を引く, 強調する 名下線, アンダーライン

☐ **undertook** 動undertake(引き受ける)の過去

☐ **underway** 形航行[進行]中の

☐ **unemployment** 名失業(状態)

☐ **unemployment rate** 失業率

☐ **unequal** 形同等でない, 同じでない

☐ **unequal society** 格差社会

☐ **unfair** 形不公平な, 不当な

☐ **unfair termination** 雇い止め

☐ **union** 名 ①結合, 合併, 融合 ②連合国家

☐ **unique** 形唯一の, ユニークな, 独自の

☐ **unite** 動 ①1つにする[なる], 合わせる, 結ぶ ②結束する, 団結する

☐ **United Kingdom**《the –》英国, イギリス《国名》

☐ **United States**《the –》アメリカ合衆国《国名》

WORD LIST

□ **university** 名 (総合) 大学

□ **unless** 接 もし~でなければ, ~しなければ

□ **unprecedented** 形 前例[先例]のない, かつてない, 未曾有の

□ **unrealized** 形 まだ実現されていない,〔利益などが〕未回収の

□ **upon** 前 ①《場所・接触》~(の上)に ②《日・時》~に ③《関係・従事》~に関して, ~について, ~して 副前へ, 続けて

□ **upturn** 名 上に向くこと,〔景気・価格などの〕上昇, 好転

□ **urgency** 名 ①緊急性 ②しつこさ **matter of urgency**《a –》緊急を要する問題, 事柄

□ **urgent** 形 緊急の, 差し迫った

□ **used** 動 ①use (使う) の過去, 過去分詞 ②《– to》よく~したものだ, 以前は~であった 形 ①慣れている,《get [become] – to》~に慣れてくる ②使われた, 中古の

V

□ **vacancy** 名 ①空虚, 空間 ②空いた所, 空き室, 空き地

□ **value** 名 価値, 値打ち, 価格 **drop in value**《a –》価値の低下[目減り], 価格の下落 動 評価する, 値をつける, 大切にする

□ **variety** 名 ①変化, 多様性, 寄せ集め ②種類

□ **various** 形 変化に富んだ, さまざまの, たくさんの

□ **vast** 形 広大な, 巨大な, ばく大な

□ **VCR** 略 ビデオ, ビデオカセットレコーダー, ビデオデッキ (= video cartridge [cassette] recorder)

□ **vehicle** 名 乗り物, 車, 車両

□ **venture** 動 思い切って~する, 危険にさらす 名 冒険 (的事業), 危険

□ **vertically** 副 垂直に

□ **vicious** 形 悪意のある, 意地の悪い, 扱いにくい **vicious circle** 悪循環

□ **video game** テレビ[ビデオ]ゲーム

□ **Vietnam** 名 ベトナム《国名》

□ **vigorously** 副 元気に

□ **vis-à-vis** 前 ~に対して, ~と比較して

□ **visa** 名 ビザ, 査証

□ **"Visit JAPAN" campaign** ビジット・ジャパン・キャンペーン《国土交通省を中心に行われている訪日外国人旅行の促進キャンペーン》

□ **visitor** 名 訪問客

□ **vitalize** 動 ~を活気[元気]づける, ~を活性化する

□ **voluntary** 形 自発的な, ボランティアの

□ **volunteer** 名 志願者, ボランティア 動 自発的に申し出る **get someone to volunteer for** (人に) ~を志願させる

W

□ **wage** 名 賃金, 給料, 応酬 動 (戦争・闘争などを) 行う

□ **washing** 名 洗濯

□ **wave** 名 ①波 ②(手などを) 振ること 動 ①揺れる, 揺らす, 波立つ ②(手などを振って) 合図する

□ **way** 熟 **in this way** このようにして **on the way** 途中で

□ **weak dollar** 《経済》ドル安

□ **weak yen** 《経済》円安

□ **weakened** 動 weaken (~を弱める) の過去形

□ **weakness** 名 ①弱さ, もろさ ②欠点, 弱点

□ **wealth** 名 ①富, 財産 ②豊富, 多

133

量

□ **wealth gap** 貧富の差

□ **weapon** 名武器, 兵器 動武装させる, 武器を供給する

□ **weigh** 動①(重さを)はかる ②重さが～ある ③圧迫する, 重荷である

□ **welfare** 名①福祉 ②福祉手当[事業], 失業手当

□ **well** 熟 as well なお, その上, 同様に as well as ～と同様に well into the future 将来にわたって

□ **white-collar** 形ホワイトカラーの, 事務職の

□ **white-collar worker** サラリーマン, 事務系の仕事をする人

□ **whole** 形全体の, すべての, 完全な, 満～, 丸～ 名《the-》全体, 全部 as a whole 全体として

□ **wide** 形幅の広い, 広範囲の, 幅が～ある 副広く, 大きく開いて

□ **widening** 名広げること, 拡大

□ **widespread** 形広範囲におよぶ, 広く知られた

□ **willing** 形①喜んで～する, ～しても構わない, いとわない ②自分から進んで行う

□ **wipe** 動～をふく, ぬぐう, ふきとる 名ふくこと

□ **with the aim of** ～を目的として, ～のために

□ **withdraw** 動引っ込める, 取り下げる, (預金を)引き出す

□ **within** 前①～の中[内]に, ～の内部に ②～以内で, ～を越えないで 副中[内]へ[に], 内部に 名内部

□ **Without reform, there can be no economic growth.** 改革なくして経済成長なし《2001年に小泉純一郎首相(当時)が掲げたスローガン》

□ **words** 熟 in other words すなわち, 言い換えれば

□ **work** 熟 go out to work 仕事に出

かける

□ **work style reform** 働き方改革

□ **worker** 名仕事をする人, 労働者

□ **working** 動 work (働く)の現在分詞 形働く, 作業の, 実用的な

□ **working-age** 形労働年齢の

□ **working-age population** 生産年齢人口, 労働年齢人口

□ **workplace** 名職場, 仕事場

□ **world** 熟 in the world 世界で

□ **World War II** 第二次世界大戦 (1939–45)

□ **world-leading** 形世界をリードする, 世界トップレベルの

□ **worldwide** 形世界的な, 世界中に広がった, 世界規模の 副世界中に[で], 世界的に

□ **worry** 熟 have worry about ～に不安を抱く[持つ]

□ **worse** 形いっそう悪い, より劣った, よりひどい get worse 悪化する 副いっそう悪く

□ **worsen** 動悪化する[させる]

□ **worth** 形(～の)価値がある, (～)しがいがある 名価値, 値打ち

□ **write off** 〔不良債権などを帳簿から〕抹消する, 〔資産を〕減価償却する

Y

□ **year-end** 形年末の

□ **years** 熟 for ～ years ～年間, ～年にわたって

□ **yen exchange rate** 円相場

□ **yen-based term** 円ベースの条件で

□ **Yom Kippur War** 第四次中東戦争, ヨーム・キップール・ウォー(1973)

Z

- **zaibatsu** 图 財閥
- **zone** 图 地帯, 区域 動 区画 [区分] する

English Conversational Ability Test
国際英語会話能力検定

● E-CATとは…
英語が話せるようになるための
テストです。インターネット
ベースで、30分であなたの発
話力をチェックします。

www.ecatexam.com

● iTEP®とは…
世界各国の企業、政府機関、アメリカの大学
300校以上が、英語能力判定テストとして採用。
オンラインによる90分のテストで文法、リー
ディング、リスニング、ライティング、スピー
キングの5技能をスコア化。iTEP®は、留学、就
職、海外赴任などに必要な、世界に通用する英
語力を総合的に評価する画期的なテストです。

www.itepexamjapan.com

ラダーシリーズ
The Japanese Economy
日本の経済［改訂版］

2005年10月10日　初版　第 1 刷発行
2017年 7 月 6 日　　　　第11刷発行
2021年 3 月 6 日　改訂版第 1 刷発行

著　者　小林　佳代

訳　者　ジャイルズ・マリー

発行所　**IBCパブリッシング株式会社**
〒162-0804 東京都新宿区中里町29番 3 号
菱秀神楽坂ビル 9 F
Tel. 03-3513-4511　Fax. 03-3513-4512
www.ibcpub.co.jp

印　刷　**株式会社シナノパブリッシングプレス**
装　丁　伊藤　理恵
編集協力　中岡　望，Gregory Turk

Printed in Japan
ISBN978 4 7946-0652-5